ADVENTURES AND CONFESSIONS OF A
HUNTER

A MEMOIR OF A HUNTERS LIFE

JACK T. GAUDETTE

ADVENTURES and CONFESSIONS of a HUNTER
First edition, published 2019

By Jack T. Gaudette

Copyright © 2019, Jack T. Gaudette

Paperback ISBN-13: 978-1-942661-19-1

All rights reserved. No part of this book may be reproduced or transmitted in any form or by any means, electronic or mechanical, including photocopying, recording or by any information storage and retrieval system, without written permission from the author, except for the inclusion of brief quotations in a review.

Published by Kitsap Publishing
Poulsbo, WA 98370
www.KitsapPublishing.com

DEDICATION

I dedicate this book (my first and probably last) to my father, Theodore "Ted" Gaudette (1903-1989). He was a mentor to both my brother (Jerry) and myself by teaching us an appreciation and love of the outdoors, from my very first memories as a child, to when he went on his last elk hunt at the age of 80.

He taught us not only the love and ethics of hunting, but also of fishing and hiking in God's great and wonderful outdoor creation.

ACKNOWLEDGMENT

I would like to thank Jennifer Adams for her help with the initial editing of my first few chapters. She is the one who got me going on the right track.

I also want to thank Brian and Linda Hunter and Tim and Thendara Kida-Gee for their help in typing several chapters of the book.

Thanks be to Scott and Patti Mohr and Nichole Brandt for their expertise in computer skills and sentence structure.

Thanks should also go to Bruce and Janie Hinds for their encouragement and help in finding an Editor and Publisher.

Also thanks to my family and many friends who encouraged me in this endeavor.

Last, but not least, thanks to Ingemar Anderson and Timothy Meikle from Kitsap Publishing for doing their magic with this book.

EDITORIAL REVIEWS

"Jack Gaudette's memoir on a life of hunting Adventures and Confessions of a Hunter may polarize opinions. We live in a time where reader's consciousnesses are more attuned than ever to the idea of "animal rights" and a loving paean to the brotherhood of hunting live game and the philosophies informing its practices will not appeal to some. Gaudette confronts this issue head on early in the book and comes at it from a Christian point of view; he believes in the Biblical dictum that man has been given "dominion" over the animals of earth and espouses his belief that any live game slain in the course of hunting should be used to its maximum value. Yet he goes on to discuss, soon after, how he coveted a cougar hide to hang in his home. Many will have opinions about the usefulness of such decoration.

Adventures and Confessions of a Hunter may seem superficially about the ins and outs of hunting live game, a collection of stories about Gaudette's experiences during various trips, and there is a degree of truth to that certainly. The guiding spirit of the work, however, is camaraderie and brotherhood. It begins with Gaudette documenting the familial origins of his love for hunting before branching out. Much of the book's first half explores his early years hunting duck, grouse, and pheasant. He makes it clear that hunting was part of the societal fabric growing up; boys developed a love for it at an early age and learned how to handle firearms responsibly.

He later transitions to big game hunting; namely elk and deer. The familial theme continues through this stage of Gaudette's life, but lifelong friendships figure in as well. His stories about hunting experiences begin in earnest at this point. Learning how to hunt big game in an effective way is a learning process and Gaudette is unafraid to chronicle how his skills and appreciation for its difficulties developed over time. He excels describing the method of dealing with bagged game, the codes and ethos governing the hunting experience, with plain-spoken detail even non-hunters can relate to.

This is one of the hallmarks making Adventures and Confessions of a Hunter such a memorable work. The book is Gaudette's first but he shows a natural affinity for storytelling honed, without a doubt, but countless nights spent around a campfire with hunting partners. He, likewise, conveys his love for the natural world with unambiguous affection – it isn't sentimental or trite but rather born from genuine respect for the earth's natural beauty.

There are serious moments laced throughout the work, but there are moments of real humor as well and Gaudette's affection for his hunting partners is an abiding theme throughout the entire book. Adventures and Confessions of a Hunter isn't a particularly lengthy work, it doesn't need to be, but is nonetheless packed with a wealth of humanity and descriptive excellence that makes it a volume well worth returning to over and over again. It will attract more than just fellow hunters – anyone interested in personal experiences honestly rendered will enjoy this work."

- Jason Hillenburg, TheMagicPen.com

"Adventures and Confessions of a Hunter by Jack Gaudette is a short but rich memoir about one man's lifetime affection for hunting. It has a linear progression tracing his experiences from childhood into adulthood and there are parallel narrative lines laying out his development as a hunter alongside his development as a mature human being. The second half of this equation is more understated than the first but is, nonetheless, an important facet of the book's reading experience. He demonstrates a sure hand for maintaining narrative focus despite this being his first book and avoids any sort of self-indulgence that might drag down the book. His conversational prose style reflects his many years relating stories about his experiences across dining room tables and over camp bonfires, but translating that skill from such casual settings into book form isn't as easy as it seems. Nonetheless, Adventures and Confessions of a Hunter never feels belabored or overworked.

It is obvious, particularly when you take his dedication to his father into account, that his love for hunting first sparked to life within his family unit. Gaudette lovingly lays out the connections he shared with his father and other family members during his formative years as a hunter, but never succumbs to misty-eyed melodramatic views about this period of his life. His gratitude is enough and shines through during this portion of the book. Much of the book is structured in the form of stories; some are dramatic, some contain humorous aspects, but one thing that burns through each of his stories is the sense of Gaudette viewing hunting through the prism of family and brotherhood throughout his life. It is no stretch to say that this aspect of the experience means as much, if not more, to Gaudette than the actual killing of the animals.

He does an excellent job of explicating the process of hunting, cleaning, and dressing animals for both those familiar with the process and those who are not. He approaches the entire endeavor from a traditionalist's point of view; it is obvious that Gaudette is a Christian, through and through, and believes hunting is a reflection of God's natural order for man and animal alike. He falls prey a handful of times to "I remember when…"-isms that younger readers may roll their eyes at smiling, but Gaudette's voice and authorial presence is nonetheless consistently likable throughout the book. He never talks down to his readers and invites them to share these experiences as equals.

Adventures and Confessions of a Hunter isn't a weighty read contending with themes; it is a collection of stories grounded in the realities of life and has an unpretentious air any reader can appreciate. Gaudette maintains, early on, that this will likely be the only book he writes, but I certainly wouldn't object to another collection of these tales – he has likely scratched the surface of his vast experiences with this book. Anyone who enjoys books or memoirs about a love of the outdoors and human companionship will find great value in this book."

- Michael Rand, TheMagicPen.com

INTRODUCTION

As I was cautiously walking up a steep and brushy trail out of a canyon, knowing full well that a mountain lion had just walked out of sight over the rise about five minutes prior to my being there, I stepped over a two-foot diameter log and glanced to my right.

There he was, crouched down alongside the same log about 20-25 feet away, staring directly into my eyes. A full- grown adult cougar about to pounce on his next meal --- me.

On a moose/caribou hunt in north western Alaska, a partner and I were scouting out the area the day before season when we chanced upon four adult brown bears fishing in a creek.

As soon as we spotted them, they spied us also. All four stood up and walked out of the creek towards us which was about 250 feet away.

The one in the lead stood up, looked at us and let out a horrendous roar. He then hit the ground on all fours and proceeded to charge full tilt directly at us with the other three bears right along with him.

I have been blessed with many wonderful and exciting outdoors adventures that include not only hunting trips but also fishing and mountain hiking/ climbing trips also. But this book is dedicated solely to the many exciting, frustrating, scary, sad, and sometimes successful hunts of an ordinary, everyday hunter (never guided).

I believe that I have experienced as many or more varied experiences than the average hunter and have been encouraged by partners, friends and family to write this book.

After reading two books "The Heck with Deer Hunting" and "The Heck with Elk Hunting" by the world- famous hunter and author Jim Zumbo, I came to the conclusion that some of my hunts were as interesting as some of his and as worthy to pass on.

So, here is a rendition of my life as a hunter. I hope you will find the stories as interesting, helpful and as exciting as they were to me.

Content

CHAPTER 1
CHILDHOOD MEMORIES — 1

CHAPTER 2
MY FIRST YEARS of HUNTING — 5

CHAPTER 3
MAKING the SWITCH FROM BIRD HUNTING to BIG GAME — 13

CHAPTER 4
BIG GAME HUNTING — 16

CHAPTER 5
MONTANA HUNT — 27

CHAPTER 6
BEAR HUNTING — 33

CHAPTER 7
COUGAR and BOBCAT EXPERIENCES — 42

CHAPTER 8
MOOSE and CARIBOU HUNTS — 49

CHAPTER 9
YEAR of the FOX — 63

CHAPTER 10
YEAR of the DOG — 68

CHAPTER 11
YEAR of the BLIZZARD — 79

CHAPTER 12
YEAR of the HELICOPTER — 87

CHAPTER 13
RARE PHENOMENA and BEAUTY — 92

CHAPTER 14
MY WORST and MOST EMBARRASSING HUNTS — 95

CHAPTER 15
FRIEND, GIRLFRIEND, BOYFRIEND — 103

CHAPTER 16
USING HORSES — MY FIRST and LAST TIME — 106

CHAPTER 17
LESSONS LEARNED and to be LEARNED — 110

CHAPTER 18
THE PAST SIX or EIGHT YEARS to PRESENT — 119

CHAPTER 19
FUN and INTERESTING THINGS — 124

CHAPTER 1

CHILDHOOD MEMORIES

From my very first memories, I can recall my father leaving and returning home from his annual hunting trips. He always seemed to have an exciting or interesting story or two, to tell us.

One story that comes to mind was about one of his partners who awoke in the morning and was putting on his boots when he discovered that a pack rat had raided their groceries and filled one of his boots with beans. Dad and another partner thought that it was a great joke and were of course giving him a pretty bad time about it. Dad then started to put his own boots on and discovered that he also had a pretty good supply of beans in his too. It wasn't quite so funny then.

Another time dad was hustling down an old logging road that was covered with ice when a big bull elk jumped out in front of him. Dad tried to stop and bring his rifle up for a sure shot since it was so close, but his feet slipped on the ice and he went down on his tail end, and by the time he recovered, the bull had disappeared.

There are numerous other stories I could tell about my father and his hunting experiences and maybe even write a book about them, but at this point I will tell you a little bit about his life.

He was born in northern Minnesota and lived on a homestead in southern Saskatchewan, Canada, until moving back to Minnesota while still a child. He left home at the age of 16 and joined the navy. While in the navy he learned the art of boxing and after his term of service was up, he became a professional, becoming the welter weight champion of Minnesota and a couple of nearby states during the mid-1920's.

He met his beautiful bride to be (Mildred Manley) in International Falls, Minnesota. They both worked for Mando Paper Co. and were married in 1926. They were married for 63 years when he passed away in 1989.

One of his hunting and fishing partners in International Falls was the hall of fame football player (Chicago Bears fullback) Bronco Nagurski. I had the privilege of meeting and talking to Bronco on several occasions while on our biannual vacations to Minnesota visiting family and friends.

He and mom moved to Bremerton, Washington, in 1941 because of a job opportunity at Puget Sound Naval Shipyard. He became a welder and retired out of there about 1962.

In April of 1948 we moved to Port Orchard, Washington, (just across the bay from Bremerton) where I have basically resided ever since.

I lived in an apartment in Seattle (while working for the Boeing Co.) with two of my friends for about three weeks, before being asked to leave; I think my friends were too naughty.

I also spent three summers and one fall logging around the base of Mount St. Helens, staying in the small town of Cougar at Ma Schmit's Boarding House. This was before the volcanic explosion blew 1314 feet off the top of Mount St. Helens in 1980.

The only other time living away from Port Orchard was during my active army time - basic training at Fort Ord, California, and O.J.T. at Fort Irwin, California.

And, back to hunting.

Some of my fondest memories are of my dad, and mom too, taking my brother Jerry and I on many fishing and hiking trips in the Olympic Mountains, and hunting trips in both the Olympics and the Cascades. It was something that Jerry and I grew up with. It was a way of life that was completely normal and natural for us. I never knew anything different and feel completely blessed to have had a part in these experiences, which so many others have not had the opportunity to be a part of.

God created a wonderful and exciting world for us to live in and I have been blessed with experiencing a good portion of it.

In recent years there have been many people and groups that frown on those of us who hunt. They say we are cruel and blood thirsty and other distasteful names.

I believe they have either forgotten, ignored, or don't know about biblical scripture, that God gave us dominion over the animals of the earth from the very beginning. Not to be cruel or to slaughter them for sport, but to be able to use them for food and clothing. I firmly believe we should not shoot or kill an animal unless we make full use of it.

I have always wanted a cougar hide to hang in my den, and actually had the opportunity to shoot one at very close range (story in later chapter), but would not do it because I did not know you could eat cougar meat. I have since tasted it, and found it to be quite good. Although my wife (Elaine) says she will not eat a cat.

For those who criticize hunting, I wonder if they really know how store-bought meat is raised, and about the slaughter houses and their techniques in killing and butchering. Also, about the quality of the meat and about the additives and preservatives that are used. Wild game is probably the most organic and heart healthy meat one is able to obtain. Also, a quick kill shot is probably more humane than practices that some butchers use.

I can remember camping with, and following my dad and brother (two years older than I) around the woods for years, before I got my first hunting license at the age of 13 (1955). At that time, you could get a license at 13 (in Washington State) but had to have a licensed adult with you while hunting. I remember at age 15 you could hunt on your own unsupervised.

Living in the country as we did, sometimes we bent the rules a little bit. We had been brought up to shoulder responsibility and to be somewhat independent, if our parents thought us responsible enough. My mother was overly cautious most of the time, but my father mostly gave us a free reign after we showed we could handle ourselves as he saw fit. He was an avid hunter, and so encouraged Jerry and I to follow in his footsteps.

I have to say that I have been an okay hunter, but brother Jerry has far exceeded my skills and successes.

So, even though I was only 13 when I purchased my first license, I was allowed to hunt on my own most of the time. My father had mentored me for years, taught me to shoot, to be aware and sure of my target, and some of the skills needed to be successful. One thing about hunting is that you are always on a continual learning scale. Every season you seem to learn new skills and lessons.

Family - (left to right) My mother, son, father, wife and daughter. Deer Camp about 1974.

CHAPTER 2

MY FIRST YEARS of HUNTING

As I mentioned in Chapter 1, I started hunting at the age of 13. I had been following my father, brother, and several older friends around on their hunts for years and finally got my chance to do it on my own.

It didn't take me long to figure out that there was a lot more action with bird hunting than with deer or elk hunting.

I think I bought my first deer tag at the age of 16 or 17, and wasn't successful at getting a deer until the age of 19. At that time, I shot a doe. In Kitsap County, they used to have a special day at the end of the regular season that they called "Doe Day." If you hadn't been successful at harvesting a buck, you were allowed a chance at shooting a doe.

I remember going out with my father and my brothers father-in-law "Em", and shooting that first deer. I was so proud, I felt about 10 feet tall. I believed I finally deserved to be called a real hunter, and that I had achieved the status of a real man.

At the time of this writing, that was the only doe I have ever taken, not that it was a thing to be ashamed of, but I always have felt I could get a buck and leave the does to birth more deer. Actually, I have been quite successful in doing this.

Well anyway, the first 8 years or so of my hunting experience, my main interest was in duck, pheasant, pigeon and grouse hunting. I would go deer hunting maybe 2 or 3 days a year, but would bird hunt about 3 or 4 days a week for the months of October, November and December. It didn't take long to figure out that if you got one shot a year at deer you were pretty darned lucky, but there were very few days that you didn't get several shots at ducks and pheasants.

I fished in the summer and bird hunted in the fall. I knew what girls were, but hadn't figured out yet what good they were or what you were supposed to do with them!

My first four years of hunting were blissful and unhampered by the thoughts of girls or their purpose. It was a wonderful and trouble-free time of my life.

Then about the age of 17 or 18, things and priorities changed. Hunting and fishing sometimes took a back seat to such things as cars and those dang pesky girl things.

Well anyway, at 13 and 14 I had a paper route that covered seven miles from home to where the paper pickup area was, a five-mile route and then back home again. I delivered the papers (The Bremerton Sun) on my bike. I had this paper route for two years.

I had an average of about 75 customers and had a huge saddlebag that I wore over my head and shoulders that had bags on both the front and back. As I said before, my main interest at this time was duck and pheasant hunting. Since my route went past several lakes, ponds, and fields, most of those fall days I would also strap on my shotgun and take it along on my route.

My first gun was an old Stevens plastic stock single shot 12 gauge. I had bought it from my brother for $15.00; and he had bought it from another neighbor boy (Lonnie Nickerson) for, I believe, $15.00 two years prior to him passing it on to me.

I would tie one end of an old rope around the barrel of the shotgun and the other end around the stock, and then sling it over my shoulder and paper bag.

Can you even imagine a kid riding down the road on his bike with a gun over his shoulder during this day and age? Besides someone calling out the swat team, my parents would probably be arrested for child endangerment or some such charge.

Times change.

I hunted mostly in two valleys (Lower and Upper Blackjack Valley). We lived on Sidney Road, which passed by both valleys.

Our house was on the south end of Lower Blackjack Valley, and about a half mile north of Upper Blackjack Valley. Blackjack Creek passes through both of these valleys, hence the name.

Back in the 1950's and 60's, and actually later, there were dairy farms in both valleys owned by two brothers (Al and Louie Riebli). They always let us neighborhood boys hunt on their farms; and actually, the game department released pheasants for several years in the upper valley, so others were allowed to hunt there also.

At the age of 13 and 14, I was hampered by my paper route to find quality time at hunting on week days; but almost every Saturday and Sunday I would leave home well before light and walk a little over a mile to my favorite spot in the Upper Valley. After sitting in my blind for about an hour, I would walk along the creek to the south end of the Upper Valley and back again. Then I'd cross over Lider Road and walk by Dunham's Pond all the way north through the lower valley, and sometimes over to Berry Lake and Beauty Lake, and then back home again. This usually covered between 5 to 7 miles, depending on my route.

I was extremely happy and proud if I brought home even one duck or pheasant. My parents always made me feel proud or worthy with even the smallest bit of success. I have to say that the few birds I brought home were not because of lack of game. It was totally because of my lack of skill at shooting on the wing. I was never and am still not a very good shot at a moving target. In fact, I'm terrible at it. Oh well!

As most hunters believe, success is not necessarily measured in what game you actually succeed in shooting. It is, and should be, in the quality of the time spent out in the bush, and who you spend it with. Actually, bringing meat home is a bonus.

There are quite a few different kinds of ducks in the Puget Sound area, with widgeons being the most prevalent. Mallards, goldeneyes, and buffleheads are in pretty good number, too.

My very first success at duck hunting happened one day when I happened to look down in a field below our house and saw three ducks swimming around feeding in a pond at the end of the field. I showed my mom and she said, "Go get them".

I grabbed my shotgun and ran down the road and crossed a barbed wire fence. I then crawled through a fern field and climbed under another barbed wire fence and made my way across a swampy field until I was close enough to shoot. At that time the three ducks sensed danger and had their heads and necks high in the air. It just so happened that they were all in a tight little group, so I aimed at the middle duck and pulled the trigger. I was quite astonished that none of them flew away. It so happened that all three were killed with that one shot; two mallard drakes and one hen. Not bad for my first duck kill. Never mind that they were ground- slewed, they tasted delicious and I was as proud as a peacock.

On another hunt in Upper Blackjack Valley, I snuck up on a large flock of widgeons. I had watched them land in a field several hundred yards from where I was sitting. So, I snuck up behind a fence line and when I felt the time was right, I stood up. Of course, the whole flock jumped at the same time. I knew better than to pick out one duck because of how poor a shot I was, so I pointed towards the thickest part of the flock and pulled the trigger.

To my surprise, ducks started falling everywhere. I ran out and started collecting them and wound up with six widgeons. Not too bad for one shot.

I was not always so lucky.

As I recall, my first pheasant kill was not one to be especially proud of. In fact, I have felt both sorrow and guilt about it ever since. But, at the time, being 13 years of age, I was pretty happy with myself for bringing home "the bacon," or rather, some pheasant meat.

At that time, we had a large building capable of raising several hundred chickens at a time, within a large fenced (6' high) area.

During one summer, a cock pheasant started flying into the fenced yard, and would go into the chicken coup and eat the chicken feed right along with our chickens. He grew to be almost unafraid of us, so one day my father used his salmon net, to net the pheasant while it was inside the coop. My father then proceeded to clip his wings so he couldn't fly away. The pheasant then lived with the chickens for a couple of months, while growing back his feathers.

Just before hunting season, that pheasant reacquired his flying skills and took off over the fence. Well, just one day after hunting season opened, he happened to fly back into the fenced yard. This was a huge mistake on his part, with a 13-year-old hunter looking for his first kill.

I spotted him in with the chickens, and immediately grabbed my trusty old single shot 12 gauge and walked out into the fenced area. He probably thought his trusted young chicken feeder guy was about to serve up a meal to him. But instead, he was the meal for us.

I still feel guilty about what happened in the chicken pen that day, but if I hadn't harvested him, for sure another of the neighborhood boys would have. There were about 7 or 8 boys of my age (give or take a couple of years) that all had hunting licenses and shotguns too.

Duck and pheasant hunting were my two most favorite things to do in those early years. When we were between the ages of 19 to 23, several friends and I used to jump in one of our cars (usually about 4 of us) and drive over the Cascade Mountains to Eastern Washington near Ephrata and Othello for the opening of pheasant season. It always opened at noon on a Saturday. We would leave home early Saturday morning and get there an hour or so before noon.

We hooked up with our friend, Bob Riebli, on his parents' farm. We would get organized (if that is the correct word for it) and head out into the corn and sugar beet fields. We lined up in a row about 30 to 50 feet apart, and then all started walking between the rows toward the end of the fields.

On occasion, one of us would get a shot before we came to the end of the field, but at the field's end, usually all Hades would break loose. There would be pheasants flying and running all over the place. Occasionally we would actually get one. My friends were no better shots at flying birds than me.

We never used a bird dog, except on one – and only one – occasion. We all learned our lesson on that trip.

My friend, Jack Carter, somehow attained a dog prior to our annual Eastern Washington hunting expedition. It was an Irish setter, which, in my opinion, says it all. He said he spent quite a bit of time training this dog to sit, stay, and retrieve. I believe his definition of "quite a bit of time" is somewhat different than mine and other people.

The four of us met early one Saturday morning, threw our gear and guns in the trunk of Jack's car, loaded ourselves and the trained dog in the car and proceeded on our exciting adventure.

We were all excited about the prospects of our bagging a ton of birds on our two-day trip, and what we were going to do with all the meat we were going to bring home. Of course, as in all day dreams, each of us were wishing and hoping that we would have the hot gun and be the hero of the trip. The other three lowly poor shots would be so jealous, and when we got home the stories would, of course, spread all over the town of Port Orchard. Well, enough of that nonsense.

We were just a few minutes down the road on a three-and-a-half-hour trip when a horrible smell spread throughout the car. Of course, we each denied that we were the culprit. I knew that each of my lowlife friends were capable of producing such a smell, especially after a night of debauchery, of which they were usually guilty.

The air had just cleared to a survivable mode, when it happened again and again and again. As stupid as we were, it didn't take a rocket scientist to figure out the source. It was Jacks well-trained dog. He had obviously forgotten to teach it any toilet manners.

That d#*# dog gassed us all the way to Riebli's farm. Three and a half hours of suppressing the gag reflex. I can't even express how horrible it was.

We finally arrived at Bobs parents farm about 15 or 20 minutes before noon, which was the opening of pheasant season.

Four excited hunters and that wonderful dog (which we all wanted to use our first shot on) piled out of the car. As soon as that dog hit the ground, it took off like a rocket. It headed straight out into the corn field at a dead run. Jack was screaming his head off at his well-trained hunting dog to come back to him.

He must have forgotten to teach the word "come" to his wonderful dog. I cannot print the words he used to express his "love" and "pleasure" with his delightful canine. The rest of us had mixed emotions about the turn of events. We had put up with that horrible creature all the way over to Eastern Washington with the hope of at least being paid back by a dog that would help us get a few more birds. The flip side was that with the dog running away, we might have a pleasant trip home the next day.

We hunted until dark on Saturday and from morning until early afternoon on Sunday, without ever catching a glimpse of that dog. We were all ecstatic (except Jack) about not having to endure the trip home with that canine septic tank. We loaded up our guns and pheasants, climbed into the car and were just pulling out of the driveway and guess what? Out of nowhere that wonderful dog came bounding into the driveway.

We had no choice but to put him back in the vehicle and head for home.

He farted all the way home.

No more dogs!

About 1956 - Six widgeons with one shot.
Myself on the left and the neighborhood boys on the right.

About 1962 on the Riebli Farm in Othello, Washington.
(Standing left to right) Myself and Marv.
kneeling left to right) Buzzy, Bill and Bob.

CHAPTER 3

MAKING the SWITCH FROM BIRD HUNTING to BIG GAME

I had been pretty much carefree and was responsible for nothing more than holding a job, bird hunting, fishing, hiking, and carousing until my 23rd year. That is when I met the love of my life, the wonderful and gorgeous Elaine Bratten, who became my wife in 1968.

I was 26 at the time of our marriage, working at the Boeing Airplane Company print shop, usually 7 days a week and working mostly 12-hour shifts. Not a lot of time to do many outdoor activities. During those 6 years at Boeing, hunting and other activities mostly took a back seat to my work and marriage.

In 1971, I got tired of commuting by ferry to Seattle, which added a couple more hours to my long day. I didn't want to live in Seattle, so took a job with Kitsap County Public Works in the traffic maintenance department. Instead of a 12-hour day at Boeing, I now had an 8-hour day with about a 20-minute commute. What a huge difference!

At that period of time I was able to resume my recreational activities with my wife's blessing – and sometimes without. Marriage can be "interesting" sometimes and sometimes not! I have to say; I have a very devoted, understanding, and faithful wife to have put up with some of my shenanigans and selfish ways. As of this writing, we have been married for over 51 years. There is a God, and He has been good to me, in spite of myself.

I should mention the fact that on our first date I picked her up at her parent's house with about 3 of my "friends", and we spent the day at an illegal cockfight. She was quite shocked and not too thrilled with that choice of a date; especially our first. You have to know it's a fact that if you start a relationship at the very lowest point, there is only one way for the relationship to go! It has to improve! She stuck with me for whatever reason beyond mine or anybody else's understanding. Maybe, she doesn't like boredom, which our relationship has not been. We also have an understanding that she doesn't have to go hunting, fishing, trapping, killing, or any other distasteful thing, and I don't have to go shopping. It works well for us, although she does enjoy going for the weekend that we set up our deer and elk camp. Well anyway, back to the hunting stuff.

Sometime after our marriage, I was influenced by my father and brother to do more deer and elk hunting. Also, I finally made the decision that I didn't care much for the taste of duck or pheasant, and so thought, "Why am I killing these beautiful creatures when I don't especially care for their meat?" Also, I observed my father doing pretty well at deer and elk hunting in the Cascades near the Oak Creek game area. My brother also was getting his deer every year on the early high hunt in the Cascades and his elk almost every year near the town of Forks, Washington. At one point, I believe Jerry harvested an elk 13 years in a row.

After giving up on bird hunting for which I believe were for very moral and ethical reasons, I became very interested and involved with the pursuit of deer and elk. There are some acquaintances that might call me obsessed or fanatic about my interest in hunting, but you have to know these people don't really understand the real-life experiences we hunters have the advantage of experiencing. Just to mention a few things like: 1) the physical exercise we get; 2) the chance to harvest healthy meat for your family instead of buying unhealthy and chemically treated meat from stores; 3) the total camping experience we enjoy; 4) Developing lifelong friendships with partners you can trust and enjoy; and 5) Sitting around a bonfire and telling stories time and again (some of them mostly true). This list could go on and on, but you hunters know what I am trying to say.

About 1976 - Myself with a spike near the town of Forks, Washington.

CHAPTER 4

BIG GAME HUNTING

After making the decision to hunt deer and elk instead of ducks and pheasants, I had a lot to learn. Although both brother Jerry and I hunted with our father numerous times, we both mostly went our separate ways as to the location we hunted.

After hunting for several years in western Washington where it rains quite frequently to say the least, dad switched over to the Yakima area. He started hunting in the Oak Creek drainage at several different locations until finally in the 1950's, settled on a remote area accessed by 4-wheel drive vehicles only, until recent years. When he first discovered this spot, he had to drive up a creek bed, then across some steep and rocky terrain until arriving at a ridge line coming off of Bethel Ridge and extending south toward the White Pass highway.

In this day and age, his off-road activities would never be allowed, but part of his original route is now an established road. I have to say that another local hunter at the time (Harry Whitehouse) was also involved in establishing this road. Dad then established his camp at this spot and hunted both deer and elk there every year until his 80th birthday. He had numerous partners throughout this time including his brother Lawrence and sister Irma, who drove all the way from Minnesota to spend 2 to 3 weeks hunting with him.

Jerry hunted with dad on numerous occasions, but eventually went out on his own with partners Pat and Milky, and hunted the Dickey Lake area near Forks, Washington for elk. He had different partners who went on the early high hunt for deer in the Cascade Mountains. His main partners on the high hunt were Leanord Paulson, Farsan

Farivar, Ron Jensen and Jerry's son Paul. After learning both areas, he did exceptionally well for both deer and elk. As I mentioned earlier, Jerry at one period of time, shot a bull every year for 13 years in a row. Then sometime in the 1990's the game department changed the area to 3-point or better area and made it a lottery draw only, to hunt there. He then had to establish a new elk area and has not been quite so successful since, although he still does better than average. He still gets his deer almost every year on the early high hunt in the Cascades.

Initially, I was not as dedicated to hunting as my dad and brother. They would take several weeks of vacation each year to hunt, and concentrate on specific areas, to familiarize themselves as to the location and activities of the local game. I, on the other hand, would only hunt weekends, and a different location every weekend. At that time, elk season was two weeks long and was the same throughout the state. Sometime later, in the 1990's, the game department shortened the general elk season to one week and gave you the choice of four areas to hunt. You had to make a choice to hunt in only one of them. Western Washington, the Yakima area, the Blue Mountains, or the Colockum area. They now have changed it again to only two areas, either Western or Eastern Washington. The general deer season has also been shortened to one week in Eastern Washington, but two weeks in most of Western Washington. One good thing is that one deer tag is good in all parts of the state. The Washington Game Commission has micro-managed our game laws so much that it can be very confusing as to what and where you can hunt. I can't speak to other states, but I would hope their laws are not as confusing. Well anyway, when I first started to take big game hunting somewhat seriously, I would hunt the first weekend with my father at Oak Creek, then the middle week somewhere in the Olympic Mountains with a friend, Ed Manning, and then the final or third weekend with my brother in the Dickey Lake area. It should be fairly obvious that I was not able to get to know any of these three areas well enough to be very successful… of which I wasn't.

I bagged a few deer and a couple of elk during this transitional time, but didn't start being a lot more successful until I chose just one area to hunt for both species. I chose to hunt where my father hunted up the middle fork of Oak Creek. His camp was and is about 14 miles up from the White Pass highway on a forest service road. There were several reasons why I chose this location instead of the Olympic Mountains. The first reason was that I was able to spend more time with my father; the second was that I did not have to put up with the rainy days in the Olympic Mountains. The third was I enjoy hunting open terrain more than thick brush; the fourth was that dad had all the necessary camp gear and the fifth reason was that dad was an excellent camp cook and furnished almost all of the groceries. All I had to do was show up, hunt, eat, sleep, do the dishes, and cut firewood.

I hunted the middle fork of Oak Creek with my father and his partners until he gave up hunting at the age of 80. I then started my own camp at the same location with two very good friends, Jim Eagleton and Bob Wilson. Jim had migrated from Wyoming many years earlier and was a very experienced hunter and is a jack-of-all-trades, plus he can cook too. Cooking is a prerequisite to being one of my partners. I do not care to cook and in fact am quite poor at it. I do the dishes. Anybody, no matter who, can be the cook. Even if there is a child in camp, he or she cooks and I'll do the dishes. I have been quite lucky that both Jim and Bob are both excellent cooks. Bob's younger brother, Bill, who joined our camp in 1980, is now the main camp cookee. Bob and I worked together for the Kitsap County Public Works Department and became best of friends right away. The first year that he worked for the county we started hunting together and continued to do so until he retired in 2010 and moved to Montana. Soon after we met, he joined me as a partner in my tree service business (topping and falling trees). We worked together at this moonlighting job until several years before he retired. I am still climbing trees, but it isn't quite as easy as it used to be.

Jim, Bob, and I hunted several years together before Bob asked if his baby brother, Bill, could join our camp. Both Jim and I, without hesitation, said "yes" because we thought he might be as valuable a partner as Bob was. Boy, were we mistaken! The first two or three years he hunted with us, I wouldn't have given 2 cents for him. In fact, I was hoping he would give up and stay home. He had some hunting experience before joining our group, but I believe that bird hunting was all he had done, so deer and elk hunting were a new experience for him. I also believe that car camping was all he had done before getting involved in an established camp, such as ours, so he had many things to learn about camp etiquette and responsibilities. He was never lazy, but needed direction in what to do and what not to do. As I recall, the first time he deer hunted with us, we sent him down toward what we call the "Flat top", which is directly below camp and on a lower rim of what we call Joe's Canyon (our own name for it). Bob and I also went down into the canyon at different locations, though Jim, usually stayed out of the canyons and usually hunted on the upper plateau.

That evening we were all having a beer around the campfire before dinner, discussing and cussing what we had seen or not seen. Right off the bat I mentioned that I had found a pile of fresh human "scat" deposited right in the middle of the trail coming out of the canyon. I could not believe that anybody with any sense at all would have done such a thing. Any normal human being would have stepped off the trail a-ways, out of site of the main trail, and deposited his waste, and covered it up one way or another. Bob, Jim and I all voiced our displeasure and shock about what had happened.

Right away, Bill spoke up and said, "O, that was me". At least he didn't lie about it, because he thought it was perfectly OK. As I said before, Bill needed some direction and training in outdoor etiquette.

Brother Bob told him in no uncertain terms that he would immediately go back down there first thing in the morning and rectify the situation. The next day when I used that same trail, it was perfectly clean. That was Bill's first camp lesson.

His next lesson came within a day or two of the first one. As I said before, Bill is not lazy and was eager to do his share of camp chores. He decided that he was capable of splitting fire wood with my father's splitting maul. He at least tried. He managed to split the maul handle, after just a few whacks, instead of the wood itself. His second lesson was that the maul head was used to hit the wood, not the handle.

Well anyway, Bill continued to learn. At that time, he was a student at Central Washington University studying to become an accountant, of which he has done very well, and so was only able to hunt weekends. I do not remember when he shot his first deer, but I do remember his first elk kill.

Bob and I had left camp the evening before and driven down to a friend's (Roger's) cabin on the Chinook Pass Hwy. to hunt and stay with him and his wife (Helen) for a day. We arrived at his cabin after dark and both had a real bath instead of the sponge type. Helen also treated us to a wonderful pre-Thanksgiving dinner complete with turkey, mashed potatoes, gravy, and even pumpkin pie. It was absolutely delicious.

The next day Bob, Roger and I hunted the Manastash Ridge area which neither Bob nor I had ever been to before. We had a great hunt but were not successful in bagging any critters. At the end of the day, Bob and I said goodbye and thank you to Roger and headed back up to our own camp arriving well after dark.

We had left Bill alone to fend for himself while we had visited and hunted with Roger, and so didn't know quite what to expect when we got back at camp. As we drove up to the tent, we were quite surprised to see that it was as dark as the ace of spades, with no lanterns lit, or not even a bonfire burning. As our headlights swung around to a little different area, there stood Bill, not moving, with his clothes almost completely covered with blood. It was really really scary. My first thoughts were "how could he be standing up after losing so much blood?" Bob and I jumped out of the truck and hurried over to him and found out that it wasn't his blood at all, but from his first elk kill. Thank goodness!

Bill had hunted by himself that morning and had returned to camp about noon. It was quite warm out so he had pulled up a camp chair and had sat down with a cold Pepsi, just enjoying the day and peaceful time, when an elk popped out of the tree line across from camp and proceeded to walk past camp and towards the edge of the cliff into Joe's Canyon.

As it was walking by, he thought he could see horns but at first wasn't quite sure. The elk got all the way to the canyons edge when he was finally sure it was a bull. He then made a good shot, hitting it in the shoulder. It jerked forward and rolled and tumbled down the shale face of the slight cliff, coming to rest about 200 feet from the top.

That's when his problems began.

He had never gutted or skinned an elk before or even seen it done, and especially on a steep rocky hillside. He soon learned that it is no easy task and especially by himself. He managed to get most of the insides out, but the skinning was another matter. He got most of the skin off but it soon got dark which made it a lot worse, so he gave up on it and just cut off a hind quarter, skin and all, and threw it on his shoulder and packed it up the hill to camp.

This accounted as to how he got so much blood all over his clothes and body. At that point he just stood around and waited for Bob and I to show up.

After Bob and I looked him over and discovered that he wasn't bleeding to death and that he had harvested his first bull we were pretty excited for him and much relieved that he was OK.

We then lit a lantern and dropped over the hill to finish the skinning and quartering, placing the meat in meat bags and packing it all out using pack boards. We then hung it all up on the meat pole so it could cool properly and be safe from any predators.

As I recall, since we were all exhausted from the long day's activities, the celebration happened the next evening.

There have been numerous times over the years that we have left a partially butchered animal on the ground overnight and finished butchering and packing the next day. So far there has been only one occasion that we have lost any meat. On that occasion, we lost only the inside loins from the result of crows pecking it out. The buck had been skinned and gutted and left lying on its back with the chest cavity left open for better cooling. Wouldn't you know that those @%#& crows would take the choicest part.

I have to add that in our camp we believe in cooling the meat as soon as possible while also keeping it as clean as possible. As soon as we get to the animal we punch our tag, bleed it as best we can, gut it, and then cut the hide away from the body, while leaving the animal lying on top of the flesh side of the hide, to keep the meat off the ground and as clean as possible. We believe that after shooting a large animal it is very important to cool the meat off as soon and as thoroughly as possible to attain quality meat.

Usually at that point the shooter will pack the head, heart and sometimes the liver back to camp. By this time, but not always, the shooter has notified the other partners by radio to get the meat sheets and packs ready for the retrieval of the meat. 90 % of the time the meat is hauled out on our backs using pack boards, although on rare occasions we have been able to drive right up to the animal. We have even shot a few animals right from the tent area, such as Bills' first bull.

In our camp it has been an unwritten rule for many years that whoever shoots a deer gets the whole deer for himself, but when an elk is harvested it is shared equally by all partners who are presently in camp at the time of the kill and/or help with the packing out of the meat. But in any case, everybody shares in the field dressing, butchering and packing out of the animal whether it is a deer, elk, bear, grasshopper or whatever, whether they get any of the meat or not. This works for us and we believe it is fair and equitable for all involved. If there are three or four hunters in camp, most deer would not provide very much meat for each individual, if divided up in that many shares, but an elk is usually substantially larger and can and should be divided up and enjoyed by all.

Another thing we do in our camp, is that whomever shoots an elk is also responsible for all of the cutting, wrapping, and distribution of the meat weather he does it himself or hires a butcher to do it. The bonus is that he gets all the glory and kudos for being the "hot" hunter, but the downside is that he is responsible for all the work and expense of butchering and wrapping.

One more story about Bill was his marriage to a gorgeous young lady named Pam Carey in 1991. Bill was as wild, uncouth, and irresponsible as just about anyone I've ever known and no way deserved a wife as fine as Pam. He eventually began to mature into a somewhat respectable character and eventually chose Pam out of all of his other girlfriends. He found a real keeper when Pam captured his heart and his life. She was and still is a beautiful girl, outwardly and inwardly, and is fun to be with and best of all she likes to hunt too. As I recall, she actually shot the first 5- point bull in our camp. Pam and their two daughters Taylor and Christa, have made a huge difference in Bill's life. Thank goodness!

When we heard about Bill's impending marriage, Bob, Jim, and myself and our wives were quite apprehensive about the success and duration of that endeavor. I believe Peggy, Jim's wife said it best when she said "I cannot believe that gorgeous girl is marrying that animal."

Well, after more than 25 years, they are still together and doing extremely well. Bill has actually become very responsible, he has developed into an excellent hunter, manages and purchases all of our groceries and equipment, and also does most of the cooking. Consequently, Jim and I couldn't ask for a better partner.

Jim and I do most of the dishes, and we all pitch in during camp setup and take down, and the cutting and splitting of the firewood. I can't imagine a better situation.

My Uncle Lawrence, myself, my father and my brother about 1978.

Three respectable 6x6 elk all shot in 2007.
(left to right) Pat Holmes, brother Jerry, and myself.

Three spikes shot in 2008. (left to right) Bill, Jason and myself.

Bob's 6x6 in 2002. (Left to Right) Craig, Bill, Jim, Greg, Don and Bob (kneeling)

My 6x6 in 2007.

CHAPTER 5

MONTANA HUNT

Although my hunting partners and myself have harvested our share of deer and elk, if not more up to the time of this writing, none of us has shot a true trophy that could be recorded in either the Boone and Crocket or Pope and Young record book. I, like most hunters would love to bag a record book trophy with the bragging rights that go along with that honor. Oh well, maybe in my next life.

The state of Washington has many wonderful and diversified locations to hunt and we have just about all the different kinds of species of big game except alligators and maybe antelope. Grizzlies and wolves are protected as well as a small band of caribou that are located in the very north eastern corner of the state.

I have read and heard that if you desire to bag a real trophy deer or elk you should set your sites on a different state such as Montana, Wyoming, Colorado, Arizona. Utah, or maybe New Mexico. Why this is, I don't know. But if you think about it, when you read the popular hunting magazines, including the "Bugle" published by the Rocky Mountain Elk Foundation, most of the stories are about hunts in the above mentioned states.

So, one year, my brother, Jerry and I made the decision to enter our names in the drawing for combination (deer and elk) general season tags for the state of Montana.

The second year of submitting our names, we were finally selected through the drawing for the hunt, as we expected. We were very excited about this hunt because we would be allowed a whole month to hunt instead of just one week in our home state of Washington.

Our first task was to decide on which area of the state to hunt.

I had no idea at all where to go except maybe near the town of Gardner because of its close proximity to Yellowstone Nat. Park and the possibility of connecting up with some of the migratories exiting the park. Jerry, however, had other ideas which was fine with me. He had a friend who lived up in the northwestern corner of the state near the town of Eureka who had been quite successful with his hunting. So, this is where we decided to start our adventure. If we were unsuccessful near Eureka after a week or so then we would head south to the town of Hamilton where he also had several friends of which we could hook up with. It all sounded good to me.

We loaded up both of our pickups with all kinds of camping and hunting gear and headed out a couple of days before the start of the general season. We located a place to set up camp, a little north of Eureka, and did just that. We cut a pretty good supply of firewood for our tent stove and a little bonfire wood also. We scouted around a bit and were ready to harvest our trophy animals the next day which was the opening of the season.

Opening morning, we set out in slightly different directions well before light. I hunted in a location where I had spotted a significant amount of fresh sign the day before. One matter of concern for me were the very large piles of bear scat that I encountered. The piles of scat were obviously made by very large bears and I was fairly confident that they were left from grizzlies, not black bears. I did not have at that time or still do not have any desire to encounter a grizzly. Thank goodness this is not a problem at any of the locations that I hunt in Washington. Another thank you is that in the time we spent in Montana, neither of us had the displeasure of meeting Mr. Grizzly. I had my share of brown bear problems in Alaska to last more than a lifetime.

Well anyway, I did not spot any elk at all on the United States side of the border, but did see a small herd across the wide cleared strip of ground on the Canadian side. I have to admit that I considered leaving my rifle on the U.S. side of the border and crossing over in an attempt to herd them over to our side, but quickly dismissed that idea.

Two thoughts made me come to my senses. The first was the illegality and unethicality of what I would be doing and the second was the fear of encountering one of those large bears without my rifle. You have to realize that bears of any size make a coward of me.

Brother Jerry passed on a nice 4-point mule deer (which turned out to be a mistake) in hopes of bagging a larger trophy and all I saw were a few smaller deer.

Probably my most exciting experience of that first week of hunting was finding an old mine shaft with a large pile of tailings in front of the cave and slightly below it. I love to explore and look for pretty rocks of which are usually of no value at all. But there is always the chance, I tell myself, that I might find the "mother lode". By far most of the rocks I pack home are classified as "leaverites" which most rock hounds know the meaning to be "leave it right there".

Anyway, in my explorations around the mine I found one rock with a couple of gold veins through it, probably fool's gold. I don't know the difference. I also found an old metal ore car with one wheel missing. I would have loved to have to have been able to get that old ore car out of the woods and back home, but obviously, it was way too heavy and far for Jerry and myself to accomplish the task.

After a week or so of no success in getting any meat, we decided to head south towards the town of Hamilton. We found a really nice place to set up camp in a large open meadow off of a road called Sleeping Child Road. Weird name for a road, but that is what it is called.

We went through the camp setup process again including cutting a large pile of firewood. We were camped right alongside a stream of which I have forgotten the name, but it was a beautiful location. Several days into our hunt there, a couple of moose ran right through our camp area. The stream next to our camp had a very fast running current and was about 15 to 20 feet across. After about a week or so there it turned very cold and that fast-moving stream froze all the way across. I was amazed. I had not experienced that before. Living in the Pacific Northwest we just do not have that cold of weather.

We hunted out of that location for about two more weeks. I liked this location much more than near Eureka. We located several excellent areas fairly near our camp to hunt. My favorite spot was a gated road that we had to walk in about a mile or so to a very large meadow area that was bordered by a barb wire fence on one side. On the other side of the fence was a private posted ranch.

In the area described above, I spotted several groups of big horn sheep that seemed totally oblivious to the fact that I was so close to them. I could walk to within less than 100 yards of them without them scurrying away. This was not a mountainous area but just a wooded meadow. Amazing! They would just keep on grazing, although a couple of rams kept an eye on me. One of the rams had a full curl which was very impressive.

There were also several mule deer in the area that I was able to get quite close to, that were very impressive also. One was a huge 4 point and the other was a 6 point that was probably the biggest deer that I have ever seen in my life up close. Both bucks in my humble estimation had to have had 30 plus inch spreads. Since that particular area was closed to mule deer hunting unless you had a special draw permit, those bucks were completely safe around me. I drooled a lot though. That area was open for white tail bucks and 3 point or better elk only. I found out later about the special draw for mule deer in that area. I wish that we would have known about the draw and about the huge bucks in that area but there was probably little chance of being drawn the one time we hunted that location. Oh well.

The closest I came to getting a shot at a legal bull was one morning when I had walked in before light and set up on a small hill overlooking two large meadows, and looking down along that private fence line bordering the private ranch. I was able to see along the fence for approximately 600 yards to a point that it disappeared over the crest of a hill.

When it got light enough to see, I spotted a herd of about 20 elk grazing and lying down right along that fence line about 450 yards from my blind. Half of the elk were on the ranch side of the fence and the other half were on the legal hunting side. You guessed it. The 6-point bull was on the wrong side of the fence. He was only about 25 feet on the other side of the fence, but he might as well have been a mile. I watched them for probably an hour or so while they were grazing and bedding, all the while considering popping that bull and wondering how long it would take me to get it across that fence onto legal land. I finally realized how wrong and dangerous to my pocket book that would be and so just stayed hunkered down and hoping that big old boy would hop over that fence into my domain.

All of a sudden, their heads came up, they stood up, and after a couple of seconds they all scurried off down and away from me. I thought what in the #%&* caused that. I looked to my left and spotted two hunters strolling along yacking at each other completely oblivious as to what was going on around them. I doubt very much if they even saw the elk or realized anybody else was even in the area. It was not the first or last-time other hunters had caused me grief. No doubt I've been guilty of the same offence.

In another area, Jerry got into a small herd and spotted a spike close enough to shoot, but since the area was 3 point or better, he was not able to pop it.

When there were only two or three days left before we were to head home, we met up with Jerry's friend and he put us on to a private farm where I shot a small 3-point whitetail. That was the only game we brought home after almost four weeks of hunting. Our trophy hunt netted us one small whitetail, but we both had a very fun and exciting time in an area we had not been to before that time. If we ever went back to those areas, we would do a few things differently but, in my estimation, it all was well worth the time we spent together and we did bring a little meat home.

A lesson to be learned is to acquaint yourself as well as possible when going to a new location to hunt.

One other interesting thing I saw while hunting on that private ranch, was watching a very small two-point whitetail buck attempting to mount a mule deer doe with a very nice mule deer buck as a spectator. The mule deer buck could have cared less about his competition.

Strange!

CHAPTER 6

BEAR HUNTING

I didn't really do any serious bear hunting until about 2004 or 2005. Of course, if I had spotted a bear in the meantime and had a good shot at it, I would have done so.

It took my good friend, Mike Hudson, to get me interested and started with this type of hunting. He was and still is an excellent hunter, and has taught me several skills in doing so. He is a much younger man but makes me look like a beginner.

He had already taken a couple of bears when he asked if I would care to go along on one of his hunts. He said that he was pretty sure he would be able to put me onto a bear. He was right. He knew where to go, when to go, and how to get close enough for a shot.

One of the things he taught me, was that you need to not only go where the bears are, but where you can see them. There are thousands of bears in the state of Washington, but because of how wooded and brushy the mountains and the lowlands are, particularly in western Washington, they can be very difficult if not impossible to see.

Again, scouting is such an important part of being successful at hunting. He taught me, even though I already had heard it before, that bears frequent and thrive in the huckleberry patches that are all over our three mountain ranges in Washington, and also, throughout the lower lands in western Wash. These berries usually ripen in the months of August and September depending on a number of factors such as the amount of rain, sunshine, and even heat to a certain extent. Since we both do a substantial amount of hiking and climbing in the mountains of our state the whole year, we have a pretty good feel for when the berry crop is ready for the berry and bear harvest.

Yes, I said berry and bear harvest. I always carry several of those large zip lock bags with me on these trips. During the hunt, I usually gorge myself on the berries and during the noon lull in hunting, I fill the bags, place them in the backpack I always have with me and bring them back to my cooler. From there they eventually make it back home for Elaine to make her world-famous pies or jam. Yum yum. It makes my mouth salivate just thinking about it.

Mike is a fireman, or I guess the official name is now firefighter. Firefighters in my estimation have one of the best jobs in the world. Yes, it can be dangerous at times, but the benefits they enjoy are amazing. He gets an abundant amount of vacation, sick leave, holidays, and what they call "K" days. I have no idea what a "K" day is, but they have them. He works 24 hour shifts and then gets 2 days off in a row. If he happens to exchange days with another firefighter, he then can get 5 days off in a row.

I said all this to show you how much free time Mike has to spend in the bush or to do whatever jerks his chain. I am so jealous of all his free time. It seems as though he has more free time than me, even though I am retired.

So, with all his free time, he has had plenty of time to explore and locate several excellent bear hunting areas. I feel honored that he has shared these areas with me and am obliged to not give any details as to their exact locations. I believe most accomplished hunters have their own private "honey holes".

I will say that my two favorite areas are in the Cascade mountains. One is just off the Chinook Pass Highway and the other is a ways south of the town of Randle.

The first hunt Mike took me on, totally hooked me into the sport of bear hunting.

One afternoon we packed up our gear and drove to one of his favorite spots. We slept in the bed of his pickup, got up well before light, had a light breakfast, and proceeded to hike up a blocked off road. We walked about a half mile or so then cut up through some woods and berry bushes until we came to the edge of a canyon overlooking several large meadows filled with huckleberry bushes. He left me at a primo spot and then headed up the rim for another 200 or so yards and set up there.

When it lightened up, I found myself looking down into a large bowl full of berry bushes and some trees surrounded on three sides by cliffs or steep banks. One side sloped down towards the road we had driven in on.

Right off the bat I spotted several small groups of elk and several deer feeding along oblivious to all else but the groceries they were gnawing on. I could hardly believe the amount of game I was seeing below me. I was glassing the area for a short time when all of a sudden, Mike showed up beside me.

He said "Do you want a bear?"

I said "Yes."

He said "Come with me."

We snuck up the canyon rim keeping back away from the edge until we got to the spot he had been watching. We cougared over to the edge of the rim and peeked over. Sure enough, there about 250 yards away was a dandy bear gorging itself on huckleberries.

Since the bear was a little farther away than I felt confident with the shot we decided that I should walk further up the "U" shaped canyon, cross over the top and walk down the other side which would bring me closer to the bear.

I hurried up the side, crossed over the top, and was ready to drop down the other side of the canyon when I discovered another bowl canyon on the opposite side of the ridge line I was about to head down. Lo and behold, there was also a good-sized bear in that bowl, too. He was as big or possibly larger than the first bear we had located.

What to do?

Since we did not have radios and I was so far away from him at that time, I made the decision to try for the second bear and let

Mike get the first one.

The bear that I was going for seemed to be in a hurry to vacate the premises. He was moving right along at a fast walk heading for some heavy tree cover. He must have picked up my scent, seen me, or at least sensed something was amiss. I should have laid down and taken a solid rest for the shot, but instead I got in a hurry and just took a knee and rested my rifle on the other knee which is shaky at best for me, especially since it was about a 200-yard shot.

I sighted on his right shoulder and fired. He took off like blue blazes and never looked back. He was in and out of trees and brush so fast that I couldn't get off another decent shot. He ran about 150 yards or so and then disappeared into a large wooded area. I dropped down into that bowl and went directly to the spot he had been when I took my shot. I found his tracks in the sand and proceeded to look for blood or hair. Nothing! I proceeded to follow his tracks as best as I could toward the tree line looking very carefully for any sign of blood but found none at all. I then walked very slowly and cautiously into the trees, going around in circles and getting quite a ways into that thick brush under the trees. I have to admit, I was very nervous about the whole episode, maybe even scared, but I would never admit that. I was schooled in the belief that if a hunter shoots at a critter, he had better be darn sure that he doesn't leave a wounded animal in the brush without making every effort to locate it.

I finally disgustedly decided that I had missed my shot. I am a terrible shot without taking a solid rest, always have been, always will be. I know very well to take a solid rest when possible, but I sometimes get in too big of a hurry. If I use a rest, I am a very good shot, but without it, I stink.

Anyway, I finally left those woods and walked back over to the ridge line I was originally headed for in the first place. Lo and behold that first bear was still feeding and lollygagging in that first bowl.

It stuck its head up out of a huckleberry bush about 100 yards away and presented a fine shot for me. I squeezed off a shot and it took off running. I took a couple more quick shots and it dropped about 50 or 60 yards from where I had taken my first shot.

My first bear. YEH!

We figured it was about a three-year-old barren female. We gutted, skinned, boned out the rib cage, and packed her down to camp. We then put the meat in a large cooler. The next morning, we went back to the same bowl and spotted two smaller bears that Mike passed on. They weren't big enough to suit him so we went home that afternoon. I was so excited to have seen four different bears in a day and a half. I was totally hooked on bear hunting.

I have heard many stories about how bad, bear meat tastes and about how greasy it can be, but I am telling the truth about this. That bear meat was so tender that you could cut it with a fork and the taste was delicious (kind of sweet tasting). It probably had something to do with the age of the bear and its diet of huckleberries. Also, it was gutted and skinned within an hour of the kill. This allowed the meat to cool very quickly, which I believe has a lot to do with the taste and quality of the meat.

Mike showed me several other areas to hunt bears over the next couple of years, and we almost always saw several quality bears each trip. He bagged another decent bear on one of those trips, but I didn't connect again until several years later on a trip by myself.

One week in late August, I decided to make a solo trip to a location off of the Chinook Pass Hwy. Although I had never seen a bear in this area, I always saw elk, deer, and mountain goats and had heard from other hunters and hikers that bears were certainly in and around there. I always enjoy hunting that area because of the magnificent scenery and the abundance of huckleberries. Great views of Mt. Rainier and Mt. St. Helens and plenty of berries to munch on.

I left home one afternoon, arrived at a small camping site, set up a car camp and spent the night. I woke up, had a quick breakfast, and was on my way well before light. I arrived at a great location overlooking a large basin that held a large berry patch plus a couple of small ponds. A year or so earlier, at this same location on a bear trip, I had been watching a small elk herd feeding out of some timber when to my great surprise an albino cow showed up. It was almost totally white except for the typical tan area around the tail and a few other tan spots on its body. What a treat that was. It was the only albino I have ever seen.

Anyway, it wasn't long before I spotted a nice bear feeding up a hillside just off to my left about 500 yards away. I quickly left my blind and headed over that way in hopes of getting a lot closer. I walked very slowly on a trail just below the hillside I had seen him headed for. All of a sudden, he popped up out of a berry bush and stood up only about 100 feet away, just staring at me. I raised my rifle very slowly to my shoulder knowing I would not have the opportunity to find a shooting rest for it and would have to shoot offhand, which everybody and their dog knows I am horrible at doing.

As soon as my rifle touched my shoulder, he dropped down on all fours and quickly beat feet back in the direction he had come. I could have chanced a quick shot, but wisely decided against doing that for two reasons. The first being my poor shooting offhand and the second reason was, I figured he would be back to that berry patch within the next day or two at which time I might get a better shot. I was correct with this assumption as it turned out.

I looked around for that critter for about a half hour or so then decided to head off further up the trail to the next big bowl about a half mile or so away.

When I arrived at the rim of the next bowl, I immediately spotted two bears grazing in a small berry patch about 1200 to 1500 yards down towards the bottom of the canyon. Since I had two more days before Elaine expected me home, I decided to drop down about 1000 yards or so and try to get within shooting distance of those big old bruins. If perchance I was able to bag one of them, I figured that I would have just about enough time to butcher, pack out, break camp and drive home (about 3 hours) before Elaine would get worried and do something about my absence without leave. Either get a rescue started or else go find a new husband. I'm sure that at times the choice could go either way depending on how pleased or not she was with me. I would like to think that she would choose the rescue option.

I went back towards the ridge on my right that dropped down towards where they were. This is a very treed ridge that allowed me to stay out of sight and downwind of them.

I got to a spot about 300 yards above them when I made another discovery. Besides those two bears, which I guessed to be about three years old, there was a sow with two cubs, feeding in the same berry patch as the two bears I was stalking, about 150 feet or so from them.

That was pretty exciting seeing six bears in one morning, considering that I had not ever even seen one bear in that area. I had known they were in the area but had never chanced on even one before this occasion.

I then dropped down towards all five bears, cougaring along behind small swales, trees, and rocks in an attempt to get as close as I could without spooking them.

I finally got to within 125 yards or so of the bears and made the decision to take the nearest three-year-old. I would never shoot a cub or a sow with a cub, of which I have passed on several occasions.

All five bears seemed oblivious of my presence. I tried to find a decent rest for the shot but was only able to find a thin wobbly sapling. I took aim as best as I could and pulled the trigger. You can guess the results. That bear didn't even flinch or anything except take off at a dead run up the hill and away from me. I again couldn't believe that I had missed again. As any decent or responsible hunter needs to do, I headed up that brushy hillside to see if I could find any blood or sign that I had somehow hit him. I walked down and then up to where he had been at the time of the shot and upon arriving at that spot, there stood the other three-year-old only about 100 feet or so away from me. It would have been an easy shot for anybody except me, but since I had shot at the other one (they were slightly different colors), I had best make sure he wasn't lying around dead or wounded before attempting to shoot a different bear. It wouldn't be too good having two bears and only one tag.

The second bear eventually waddled off which allowed me to make my search for the first bear. I walked all over that hillside searching and thrashing around trying to locate even a sign of that first bear without finding any blood, hair, tracks or anything at all of him. One very strange thing occurred. That sow with the two cubs continued grazing in the same spot, maybe only 150 – 200 feet from where I was noisily searching for the critter that I had shot at. I searched for quite a while before finally giving up and getting the heck out of there. That mama and her babies had me somewhat spooked. I again was thoroughly disgusted with myself.

I got back to camp after dark, ate, slept and was up and on the trail again before daybreak. Just at first light, I was approaching that first bowl where I had spotted the first bear the day before. Sure enough, there on that hillside where I had passed up that quick 100-foot shot, was that same bear feeding in that same berry patch just like I had thought he would be.

This time I snuck up to the top of the hill and out and down to a rock outcropping above him. I laid down and rested my rifle on a big rock, put the crosshairs on his right shoulder and nailed him. Like I've said before, if I have a good solid rest my shooting improves considerably. I hope he enjoyed that last mouthful of huckleberries.

Anyway, I gutted, skinned, boned, and packed him out by early afternoon. He wasn't a very big bear, probably the first year away from his mama.

I still had several hours of daylight left and was still wondering and concerned about that bear I had shot at the day before in the further canyon. One of my biggest fears is about wounding an animal and having it crawling off and dying someplace without being found. I believe that it is a moral and ethical issue for hunters to be concerned with. We need to be accountable for our actions.

So, I then hustled about a mile and a half to that far canyon and glassed down to where I had seen the five bears the previous day. Much to my relief, I spotted all five bears still grazing in that same berry patch they had been in the day before. Yahoo, I must have cleanly missed him. What a relief to know I'm a terrible shot.

There is a nonprofit Christian organization based in the city of Tacoma, Washington called "Network" that has a charity auction where services and items are auctioned to help fund the organization. Network aids the poor who are trying to get back on their feet. The organization provides temporary homes, food, vehicles, and some job opportunities to help them become self-supporting again. The recipients are closely monitored and given counseling on making life changes that will help make them self-sufficient. Elaine and I believe it to be a worthwhile organization and have been supporting it for a number of years.

The reason I am mentioning this, is because I was talked into offering a bear hunting trip. Not really a guided hunt, because there is no way I could ever be considered a guide. But I can furnish the entire camp equipment, furnish the food, and let the winning bidders suffer with my cooking skills. NOT! And there is a possible chance that I could actually locate a bear for them to get a chance at.

The trip sold out the three years that I offered it, to my great surprise. I consider it a win win situation whereby the "clients" get a nice hunting and camping adventure, Network gets a few dollars to help the poor, and I get another trip to the mountains. How can you possibly beat that?

So far, all the "clients" have seen elk, deer, mountain goats, and gorgeous countryside, but no bears. Still, I believe they all enjoyed the outings as much as I sure as heck did.

CHAPTER 7

COUGAR and BOBCAT EXPERIENCES

I truly believe that hunters should not kill any animal that we cannot eat, unless we or someone else, is in imminent danger because of it, or it is considered a nuisance and causing damage to farms or domestic animals.

I have been blessed with seeing (while hunting) three cougars and five bobcats. I would guess that the majority of hunters have never seen even one of these critters in the wild.

My first cougar experience was a very exciting and somewhat scary situation. About 10 or 12 years ago, I was elk hunting out of our camp in the Oak Creek Game Range. I had hunted down into a canyon below ours and the Jim Jim's camp. Also, below what we call Bobs Meadow. Bob shot his first bull there the first year he hunted with me in 1985, hence the name.

I was pussy footing along a well-used game trail below that meadow, when I suddenly heard elk calling to each other just below me and only 100 or so feet away. The trees and brush were quite thick, so as they beat feet downhill, I was only able to catch a few glimpses of legs and butts as they descended toward what we call Fish Flats. Anybody, even non-hunters, who have spooked an elk or especially a herd would recognize the unmistakable smashing and crashing noise they make while exiting an area in a panic.

I had heard that it was possible in some instances, to run alongside a herd of elk, and if they didn't actually see you, they might mistake your sound as one of their own and come towards you or at least not shy away. So, considering I didn't have too much to lose, I took off running down the hill for quite a ways. Well, it didn't work.

I shortly lost all contact with them and found myself down that canyon further than I wanted to be. I hunkered down a bit and then started walking back up the very same trail.

I was walking back up the trail very slowly, when I spotted an animal standing crossways on the trail about 150 feet away. My first impression was that it was a small deer because of its short height and the brownish color. On second glance, I realized that a deer does not have a three-foot-long tail. I stood in complete dismay, realizing that what I was looking at was a full-grown adult cougar. I never dreamed that I would experience seeing one of these magnificent creatures in the wild and having it SO CLOSE. I know only a handful of hunters who have ever seen one of these critters without the use of hounds. I cannot fully explain how thrilled and excited I was at being so lucky or blessed at experiencing that event.

I slowly raised my rifle to a shooting position, placed the crosshairs on his shoulder and touched the trigger with the safety in the on position. He was mine, if I wanted him. I had dreamed about having a cougar rug in my den for years, but I had no idea that you could eat cougar meat, and as I have mentioned before, I will not kill an animal just for the hide or sport. I am not saying it is wrong to do that, but it's not for me. Lots of hunters would justify taking a cougar because of all the deer and elk they kill for their own food, which cuts in on the amount of game left for human consumption. I fully understand that reasoning, but just looking at that magnificent animal and knowing that I could have made the kill was good enough for me.

The story is not over yet.

That cat then slowly walked up and over a little hill and disappeared while still staying on the same trail I was standing on. What to do? My only real choice was to walk on up that trail where he had just disappeared. It was way too brushy and steep on either side to detour around him. I walked very slowly up that trail (looking everywhere) to the spot where he was last seen. I continued another 50 feet or so up to where a one-and-a-half-foot diameter log was laying across the trail. I was getting quite nervous at that time wondering where Mr. Cougar had gone or not gone. I glanced along the log to my right and to my surprise, there he was, crouched down right alongside that log about 25 or 30 feet away. He was in a full crouch just staring right into my eyes.

I raised my rifle up and put the crosshairs right in the center of his face. I again placed my finger on the trigger and said to myself "You could be mine." We stared at each other for possibly a minute or so, with me totally admiring him, thinking about what a magnificent creature he was, until finally deciding that I had better be moving on.

I don't know if he was just as curious about me as I was about him, or if he was also thinking, "You could be mine for supper", or just waiting for me to move on so he could get back to doing whatever he was doing. The thought passed through my tiny little mind that he might just be waiting for me to turn my back to him so he could completely ruin my day.

I concluded that I didn't feel very safe with him so close and seemingly unafraid of me, so I snapped off my safety, took a quick short jump towards him and yelled very, very loudly.

It astonished me at how quickly he moved. He leaped about two or three feet into the air, turning in midleap in the opposite direction and disappeared over a small hill all within about two seconds. After seeing at how fast he moved, made me realize that if he had decided to come at me, I probably wouldn't be here to write this book.

I then scampered up to camp with a wonderful tale to tell without the need to exaggerate at all. It was good enough just the actual way it all came about. It seems as though when a hunter has a really good experience to tell, everything else goes on the back burner until we are able to tell our story to our buddies. That is largely what hunting is all about, the opportunity of sharing our adventures with our good friends and family members.

A year or two after this incident, I found out that you can eat cougar meat. In fact, some say it is very good. After sampling it later, I found it to be quite tasty. I then made the decision that if the opportunity ever again presented itself, I would indeed get my cougar mount plus some meat for the freezer, although my dear wife, Elaine, says she will not eat a cat.

The second cougar I had the pleasure of seeing was again in the Cascade Mountains. In the state of Washington, there is an early high buck season for rifle hunters that always starts on Sept. 15. And runs for 10 days ending on Sept. 25. It is a 3 point or better season and is held only in several areas that are in the higher elevations in both the Olympic and Cascade Mountain Ranges. Most hunters that take advantage of this early hunt use horses or mules to get into the higher elevations due to the distance and steepness of the trails to get to the areas open to the hunt.

One of my partners, Mike Hudson, and I decided to take advantage of this early hunt and since neither of us had horses, made the decision to hike in about four miles or so, by foot, with everything on or in back packs. We were in the Salmon La Sac area, which is on the eastern side of Snoqualmie Pass. This area was also open for bear and cougar, besides 3- point or better bucks.

We drove over to the east side of the mountains to the trail-head, parked our vehicle, and then hiked up and into where we established a spike camp the day before season opening. After camp setup, we just meandered around enjoying the views and doing a little scouting around for fresh sign before sacking out for the night. We arose way before light and went off in our own preferred directions so we could be set up at the crack of dawn.

I made the decision to walk out and hunt along a ridge looking down into brushy treed canyons on both sides of me. I hunted this ridge without seeing a single critter until about 10:30 or 11:00 and then slowly started back towards camp.

I happened to glass down into the canyon on my right when I noticed a movement in the brush about 200 yards away. It popped out of the brush into a very small opening, and I realized it was a cougar, just meandering along seemingly without a care in the world.

I quickly laid down and rested my rifle on a small dirt and rock mound, and sighted in on another small opening a short distance in front of and in the same direction he was headed. Sure enough, he stepped right out into that clearing and walked right into the center of my scope. I placed the cross-hairs on his left shoulder and moved along with him, making sure everything was aligned as it should be. Just as I was on the verge of squeezing off a shot, the scope went black. I almost fired anyway, quite sure the shot was aligned correctly, but thought better of it. I did not want to make a bad shot with the possibility of just wounding him. I would take only a sure shot or no shot at all.

It took me a couple of seconds to figure out why the scope had gone black. I was wearing glasses at the time, and when I was moving the gun along following that cat, the sun from behind me had somehow shined through the backside of my glasses, my scope, or maybe both causing the scope to go black. Why that happened at that time, I do not know, but it sure as heck ruined my shot. I had a good rest and everything seemed perfect, but the shot didn't happen.

I then spotted another small clearing about 100 feet ahead of where he had been. I again set up on that spot hoping for another chance at him, but he was a no show. Where he disappeared to, only the Good Lord knows.

My third cougar sighting was on a bear hunt at the same location where I had shot my first bear.

I was on the upper ridge line at the point where a lower ridge line dividing two large bowls below me intersected the ridge I was on.

I had hunted hard all morning and then found myself at this location where I could sit down and observe both bowls at the same time. I then proceeded to have my lunch, read my book, take a snooze or two, look around, snooze a little, look around and so on.

This is my favorite type of hunting. It's just wonderful!

Well anyway, at one point I looked up from my book and spotted a movement about 200 or 250 yards away. I picked up my binoculars, glassed over and down towards the movement and lo and behold, there was Mister Cougar just moseying along in a direction directly away from me. I realized right away that he would be entering thick brush and trees before I could get a decent shot at him, so I just watched him until he disappeared, which was only a couple of seconds.

I always feel very blessed when I see one of these magnificent creatures. My freezer may be empty but my memory is full.

BOBCATS

Throughout my hunting years, I have seen five bobcats but have never shot at one. As I have stated before, I will not shoot any animal that I will not eat, therefore they are quite safe around me. Every one I have seen was while I was hidden in a blind except one which happened to be the first one I encountered.

I was elk hunting in the saddle about 500 feet in elevation below our camp. The saddle is between our camp and an area or bluff that we call "the Flattop". It was just getting light enough to shoot and was lightly snowing. I was pussy footing along in about 5 or 6 inches of fresh snow just admiring how quiet and beautiful it all was. I stopped for just a few seconds looking around when I caught site of a movement on top of a log only about 60 or 70 feet away. Out of the shadows and snowflakes came this beautiful bobcat walking slowly down the log directly towards me.

I was dead still and just stood there and admired him. He slowly walked towards me and then jumped off the log and disappeared off to my left in the murkiness and falling snow. I don't think he ever knew I was there. Over the years I have seen three other bobcats in that same general area, but not as close or as exciting.

Several years ago, my friend Mike Hudson and I decided one winter day to drive up to the foot of Mt. Townsend in the Olympic

Mts. to see if we could spot a cougar, but mostly just to have a fun outing in the snow.

Several of my hiking/ climbing friends had spotted a cougar there a couple of months earlier on one of their climbs. So that was the excuse Mike and I used to go there.

There were small patches of snow at the trailhead but about a foot or so of snow at the summit. He, being more ambitious than me, decided to follow the trail all the way to the summit which was about three miles and maybe 2000 feet higher. I decided to stay close to the trailhead and watch several very large logged off clearings.

I was sitting on a stump just below the roadway looking over one of the clearings. I glanced to my left and spotted a critter emerging from some huckleberry bushes and drop down onto the road about 75 or 100 yards away from me. I realized right away that he was a pretty little bobcat on the hunt for breakfast. He walked in a direction away from me and kept dropping below the roadway and then back up again. Then he would go back above the road in the brush and then back to the road again. He continued this for about 400 yards until he finally popped out of sight over the top of a hill.

Another wonderful experience!

Mike finally returned with nothing but a story of seeing a couple of old cougar tracks. It was still a mighty fine day as far as I was concerned.

CHAPTER 8

MOOSE and CARIBOU HUNTS

I have had the privilege of taking part in three moose hunting trips, two in Alaska and one in North Eastern Washington. One of the hunts in Alaska also involved caribou hunting for two of my partners.

The first trip, which was on the shores of lake Becharof, Alaska was the most interesting and scary hunt of my lifetime.

In 1993, it all started out with several of my friends, who wanted an adventurous hunt in Alaska that was a bit out of the ordinary. Believe me they got what they wanted, and more.

Three of my schoolmates, Bill Bloomquist, Mike Moore (who lives in Alaska), and Sam Comstock, plus two other friends, Jay Weatherall and Don Holmes, got together and planned most of the trip, and then decided they needed someone else of limited intelligence along, so they invited me.

They had the trip well planned ahead of time, even to the extent of buying a Zodiac boat and sending it and an outboard motor, several cases of beer, tents, cooking gear, and other assorted items up to a town called Egegik on the Aleutian Peninsula, via a commercial fishing boat. The gillnetter belonged to one of their relatives and had left the Seattle area in the spring, and traveled up the coastline and around the Aleutian chain and thru Bristol Bay to the town of Egegik. The fishermen then offloaded our supplies at a fish processing shed until we had the occasion to pick them up in September.

The six of us obtained our hunting licenses and appropriate tags. The tags were all a little differently priced. As I remember caribou tags were $350 and moose tags were $450. If you had a moose tag, then you could fill it with a caribou if you failed to get a moose, since the caribou tag was less cost.

The five of us from Washington all flew to Anchorage together and then took a flight to King Salmon the same day. We stayed overnight there. The next day we met our bush pilot whom I will call Al, who then shuttled us to the village of Egegik.

We gathered up our supplies from the processing shed in Egegik, and Al then started shuttling us out to a spot that we picked out on the map. Al said "I hope you know what you are doing, because you will have bear problems." We all said, Haw Haw, what does he know, there are six of us with high powered rifles."

We found out who the dumb ones were, and it wasn't him.

We all got to camp at staggered times, since we and all our gear amounted to about four loads for him in his Piper Cub. As soon as the first two guys hit the ground, they located a spot and started setting up the tents. We had three tents, a large one for sleeping, a cook tent, and one to keep equipment in, such as the pack boards, extra gas for the boat and odds and ends. We had camp pretty much set up by dark. Our camp was about 300 yards from Lake Becharof and about 200 yards from Featherly Creek, which emptied into the lake. Bad location, we found out later.

That first full day in camp, which was the day before season opened, we scouted the area around the camp, which wasn't very hard to do because there were no trees, just low scrawny alder bushes about seven feet at the tallest. We fished in the creek which was full of spawning salmon, Dolly Varden and Grayling. We caught some Dolly Varden for supper. As I recall, we only had one fishing pole, but it was plenty to keep us supplied in fish.

The creek was where we spied the first bear tracks, but as of yet, we hadn't seen a bear. These tracks were bigger than any of us had ever seen. At that time, the fear had not settled in yet.

We started glassing the distant hills around us and spotted a large bull moose on a distant hill, close to a mile away. The sun was out and his large antlers looked like a mirror the way they reflected light back at us.

About that time, a plane flew in to the far end of that hill and deposited a guided hunting camp. One of my partners, Don Holmes, who was about as ignorant as I am, said "we spotted the moose first, so let's make a couple of sandwiches, grab a two man tent, our sleeping bags, guns, and walk over to the base of that hill, and camp out until season opens tomorrow."

Sounded like a good idea to me, so off the two of us went. By the way, we had to cross a large but shallow swampy area to get there, so we were wearing hip boots for the entire hunting trip, not so comfortable to be in for that much walking.

We got to a sandy, but dry area, about 150 yards from the base of the hill and set up our small tent, thinking we had outsmarted that guide and his clients. We had about an hour before dark, so we decided to walk parallel to the hill over towards the creek, which was about 250 yards from our small tent.

We got to within about 100 yards of the creek, when I spotted four large brown heads looking up out of the creek at us. Neither of us had ever seen a brown bear in the wild. As soon as I spotted and pointed the bears out to Don, I said "Let's get out of Dodge pronto."

It wasn't soon enough!

All four were adult bears. The smallest was probably about 400 lbs. and the largest maybe 500 lbs. or more. I have heard that some sows will keep their cubs for up to three years and maybe this was the case. I do know they weren't cubs.

All four bears came up out of the creek on our side, took a look at us and then one stood up on its hind feet, growled and headed straight for us on a run, with the other three on its tail.

There are no trees to climb even if we had the time, and we knew, it would be worse if we ran, so we stood there looking as big as we could, yelling and waving our arms, but they kept coming.

When they were about 100 feet away, I took quick aim at the lead bear and started to squeeze the trigger. Now, all of this happened in just a couple of seconds, and once I pulled my rifle up and prepared to shoot, it was like everything was in slow motion. Amazingly, the first thing I thought of, was how beautiful a creature that bear was. The head filled my scope as I tried to place the cross hairs between its eyes, knowing that a body shot at that distance would not kill it soon enough, before it would do considerable damage to my body.

The second thought was, "How could this be happening to me? This is something you would read about in a sporting or hunting magazine, not experience it yourself?"

The third thing I did, just before putting pressure on the trigger, I said to myself, "Help me Jesus!"

The bears immediately stopped about 40-50 feet away, they stood there for about 10-15 seconds, then turned and walked away.

Don, knowing that I had a camera on me, as soon as they stopped, he said several times, "Take a picture."

I was shaking so bad, that by the time I pulled out my camera, and took a picture of them, they were a good 100 to 150 yards away. In the picture they appear to be just brown spots on the sand.

We almost left brown spots on the sand, too.

As soon as they returned to the creek, Don and I returned to our tent, which was only about 100 yards from where we had seen the four bears. We looked up at the hill above our tent and saw five more bears about 200 yards away. They were walking down the hill towards us. We again stood tall, waving our arms and yelling at them. First one stopped, then two more, further down. The fourth one stopped at the foot of the hill, but the fifth one kept walking towards us on the sandy area. Finally, it stopped and laid down about 125 feet from us.

All this happened just at dusk. We watched those five bears until it got so dark, we couldn't see anymore. We walked the short distance, about 50 feet, to our tent, with those five bears just sitting and laying down such a short distance from us.

We got inside, head to toe, with our loaded rifles right next to us. A lot of good they would have done if one of those bears decided to enter our tent. We got next to no sleep that night. It was probably the scariest night I have ever experienced. We would have been like a big burrito to them, if they had decided to have meat for dinner, instead of fish.

Talking to the guys at base camp, which was about a mile away, the next day, we found out that they had seen five other bears besides the nine which we had seen. Fourteen bears in that small area, I think, is a little extreme. Apparently, our bush pilot friend was correct with his advice about we were going to have bear problems.

Don and I woke up alive the next morning, and went about hunting that hillside, but did not find the moose we had spotted the day before, but neither did the guide and his clients.

We returned to base camp that afternoon and found out that the other four guys had hunted out of the Zodiac, and Sam had bagged a really big caribou. They had hauled it back to a tin fishing shed about 300 yards from our camp and hung it up inside. There was one window and a doorway in the shed. They had boarded up the openings with some old lumber laying inside the shed and left it for the night.

We got up the next morning and went directly to the Zodiac, which had been left on the beach from the previous day, to find to our amazement, that it was completely destroyed, as well as the outboard gas can and lines chewed thru.

We ended up burning what was left of the boat that afternoon. Kind of expensive for only using it once.

Several bears which were always marauding around camp must have smelled the fresh caribou blood on the raft and gas can and gas lines. It was like inviting them to dinner, we should have known.

Then we went to the shed to check on the caribou meat, and found the boards ripped off and half the meat missing. A really skinny, crippled sow, with one big fat cub ran from us when we approached the shed. We salvaged and guarded what was left of the meat until our bush pilot flew in that morning. He loaded what was left of the meat and the caribou horns on his piper cub and off he went.

That same day, we again spotted that moose over on that same hill, which Don and I had hunted the first day. This time all six of us walked over to the hill and converged on him from six different directions, three on each side, two at the bottom, two in the middle and two at the top of the hill.

I was in the middle of the hill on his right side. As I was sneaking along, I spotted him laying down in a small clearing about 100 yards away. I laid down, took careful aim and shot him in the head. That was the end of Mr. Moose.

Bill and Mike started butchering him right away, while the other four of us started backpacking the meat to an open sandy area on the opposite side of the hill. We had to go up the hill and down the other side. The distance for each round trip was probably a half mile. This was no easy task wearing hip waders and carrying about 50 lbs. a load. He was a large moose with a spread of 57 inches.

We were lucky enough that the bush pilot flew in that afternoon to check on us. He spotted us and landed right where the meat was laying. After seeing the horns of the moose, I was so proud of, he said "Why did you shoot the baby? There is a much bigger one about 300 yards further up and along the hillside."

Well anyway, Al flew us back to camp, and then flew Bill and Don with a small tent and a little grub back to where I had shot my moose. They spent the night there, and Al flew my moose back to civilization to be put in cold storage. Bill and Don planned on going after that other bull the next day. There is a rule in Alaska, that you cannot hunt the same day as you fly, so they had to wait until the next day to go after him.

Sure enough, Bill spotted him the next day. He shot him, and the two of them butchered him on the spot, and then started back to camp. They were only able to carry about 60 or so pounds of meat on their backs apiece, and had to leave the rest of the meat, plus the head at the kill site.

By afternoon, a huge storm came in with torrential rain and severe wind. They still hadn't made it back to camp well after dark and the rest of us were worried sick. By this time, we had seen many more bears and with that cold, windy, and rainy weather, we could only guess what had happened to them. It would have been useless and dangerous for us to leave camp in that storm with no chance of locating them in the dark and the horrible conditions outside.

We hunkered down in the tent trying to get some sleep, but found it very difficult, with the raging storm and the worry about our friends.

Sometime around eleven or twelve that night, we heard three quick shots off in the distance. We had a quick conference in camp, and decided that two of us, Mike and myself, would head out in the storm towards where we had heard the emergency signal, and the other two, Jay and Sam would stay and guard the camp.

We had no idea what kind of problems Bill and Don were having, but there was really no choice but to go out and try to aid them.

Mike and I suited up in our hip boots, rain gear, rifles and flashlights and took off. The flashlights did little good except that we could stay together, and somewhat see where we were stepping in that swampy, tundra and brush.

We got about a third of a mile from camp when we found them. They each had a huge pack of meat, as well as the tent, sleeping bags and their rifles. They were absolutely soaked and exhausted. Mike and I were ecstatic about seeing them both alive and somewhat OK. Mike and I shouldered their packs and led them back to camp.

We dumped the meat in a large pile about 200 yards from camp in the futile hope the bears wouldn't find it. We knew better than to leave it in camp. Of course, the next day, it was all gone, and we knew that the remainder at the original kill site would be gone too, including the head and horns. Bill later said that his lost bull was in the upper 60-inch range, maybe closer to 70 inches. Too bad!

The storm blew for three days, demolishing our equipment tent, which we had to burn, and damaged our other two tents. Duct tape, rope and twine kept our other two tents together, somewhat. During the three days and nights, the bears were constantly in and around our camp. Sometimes during the night, the tent would shake violently from the bears bumping into the tie down ropes, and you could hear them huffing and sniffing right next to the sidewalls of the tent, a bit unnerving to say the least.

When the storm finally broke, the bush pilot flew in and started evacuating us. He got all of us and the remaining equipment out on that final day.

One day before the storm, Mike had also shot a small caribou, but the bears got the whole thing. A lesson we sadly learned was that there was no sense in shooting anything unless the pilot flew in that same day to evacuate the meat.

The score was; Bears 2 ½ animals, one boat, and a tent, and us 1 ½ animals. We were very good at supplying supper for them. We had a very exciting time and even fun at times, and did come away with some meat, but it was pretty unanimous that we would never ever go back to that location.

My next moose trip to Alaska about three years later, was much more successful, and quite exciting, but a zillion times less scary. This time we saw only two black bears and they wanted nothing to do with us. Thank You Lord!

There were seven of us on this hunt. Sam Comstock and I flew up from Washington to meet Mike Moore and four of his Alaska friends. Sam and I flew into Anchorage and teamed up with the rest of the party. We trailered three flat bottom river boats between 20 – 25 feet long, up through Fairbanks and to the town of Circle where the highway intersected the Yukon River.

We spent the night there, but got up very early, launched the three boats and were on our way just about dawn. This was a very long day as well as the next day also. We traveled about 350 miles down the Yukon that first day to the village of Galena. We spent a short night there sleeping in our boats, then motored a short distance further down the Yukon, turned north and travelled about 250 miles up the Koyukuk River. We finally got to our destination which was on Dolby Slew.

I remember being so excited about travelling such a long distance on the mighty Yukon River and also the more remote Koyukuk River. It was quite interesting for a while, but I have to admit, the scenery changed very little during the whole trip until we arrived at our camp.

Several interesting things I observed were the way the villagers tethered all their sled dogs apart from each other, the way they dried their fish (salmon) for dog food, and that their cemeteries were away from the villages and all seemed to be on a hillside facing to the east. The salmon were all split from their head to the tale and then draped over wood racks in the open air. There were literally hundreds of fish at each residence. I wondered about the smell, how they kept predators away, and how long they were left to hang.

Several things about this hunt were that it was considered a trophy area (no bulls with racks less than 50 inches wide were legal) and the use of airplanes was strictly prohibited. The only way to get in or out was by boat unless it was an extreme emergency. All boats had a complete supply of parts to completely repair or replace the lower units and most of the engine parts also. We also had several 30-gallon drums of gas on each boat plus the built-in gas tanks. All of these were refilled at Galena, both going to and coming back.

We set up camp and started hunting right away on what was planned to be a 10-day hunt.

The way we hunted was two to three persons per boat. We would motor up the waterway which was anywhere from 20-foot-wide, to maybe 100 foot wide and very, very, twisty. If we spotted a moose, we would beach the boat, get out and try to find it in the brush and small trees where it had trotted off. These are non-migratory animals and so would not run off too far. Most of the time we would just stop at a likely spot and get out being as quite as possible. We would then walk a short-way and try calling them in. This was done by beating the brush and trees with a boat oar and grunting in a similar manner to the sound they make. A couple of the Alaska boys could do this quite well. This was their mating season, so we tried imitating what the bulls would do when trying to lure a lovesick cow to their love nest. When we would be successful in shooting a bull, we would winch it over towards the river bank with a chainsaw winch. I think our longest winch was only about 150 yards, and most were much shorter. At that point we would chainsaw the bull into six sections, (four legs, rib cage, and neck section). We used a small chainsaw with vegetable oil in the oil tank to keep the meat clean. It worked very well. The only scary part of the hunt was when I shot my bull.

Mike, Felix (my boat partner), and I were hunting out of Felix's boat when we saw a cow moose come up, and out of the river and walk inland. We stopped, got out and walked up the bank about 150 feet through some trees and came upon a large meadow. We immediately saw the cow with a nice bull following her about 100 yards from us.

I aimed offhand at him, put the cross hairs on his ear and fired. Down he went! All right, I thought, but I noticed his butt was still in the air. I found out later that my bullet had creased him across the top of his skull.

He had been cold-cocked, but was very much alive.

He stood up and started walking parallel to us, I aimed at his eye this time and shot again. This time I could see the fur fly and his head flinched. The bullet had passed right through his cheek, but missed the brain. This must have irritated him something awful because he turned and started trotting right at me. I had crossed the line with him and he was going to make me pay. Now he was only about 150 feet away and coming fast. My third shot was aimed right between his eyes. I pulled the trigger and I could see the fur fly where the bullet hit him just below his eyes and passed thru his head and on into his chest. He kept coming right at me.

I shoot a 300 Winchester Magnum, and since it carries three bullets in the magazine and one in the chamber, I knew I had one more shot. I quickly aimed between his eyes again and squeezed off again at about 75 – 100 feet.

CLICK – The gun went click.

Stupid foolish me, I had taken the bullet out of the chamber when in the boat as a safety precaution and forgotten to put it back in. I jumped behind the nearest tree, (a three- or four-inch sapling) which would not have stopped his charge and tried to find another bullet and reload. I would not have had time, but again the Good Lord saved my buns.

The bull dropped about 25 or 30 feet before he would have reached me and skewered me with those huge horns. His horns measured 57 inches wide, the same width as the bull I shot by Becharof Lake. I might add that Felix had left his rifle in the boat and I was between Mike and the bull, hence he could not get a shot at it without hitting me. So much for my backup.

We ended up shooting seven bulls in five days. The smallest was 50 ½ inches and the largest was 67 inches.

We packed up our meat, and equipment and headed back down the Koyukuk and to Galena, where we stopped to ship our meat by plane to Anchorage, where it was put in cold storage until we picked it up to butcher it ourselves.

At Galena, we placed each moose on a separate pallet to be shipped out. The smallest moose weighed over 600 lbs. of just meat, and the heaviest one was just over 700lbs. That a lot of meat. We spent one more day on the Yukon returning to Circle and another day on the road to Anchorage.

What a great hunt!

My third moose hunt was with my brother, Jerry, in the Selkirk Area, in North Eastern Washington. There is a lottery draw in Washington for moose tags. If drawn, it is a once in a lifetime hunt. Jerry was blessed enough to draw a tag. Jerry, his wonderful wife, Alice, and I headed out one October day to Sullivan Lake, where we set up camp.

The weather was nice the first couple of days but then became very cold and began to snow. I had never been in the area before, but Jerry and Alice had scouted it out in the summer, so he had a pretty good idea where to hunt.

I was along for several reasons, Jerry had just recently had a knee operation, so having an extra hand and back along to help with camp chores and such, was one of the reasons. Also, to help scout and help pack out such a large animal would be helpful to him, and besides we are brothers. That is the best reason. We share a lot of things and spend a lot of time together. It might sound corny, but we love each other. Don't ever tell him I said that, he might vomit.

I was also carrying my rifle, because bear and deer season were open to all hunters at the same time Jerry was after his moose. Two things you should know, the first was he could also shoot a cow moose with his tag, but was determined to only shoot a bull, and the second thing was that occasionally we party hunt (which in not legal) but he told me in no uncertain terms that he would be shooting his own moose. I could help him scout one out, but I'd better not shoot it. As it turned out, I saw three other bulls before he saw and shot his first one.

One of the bulls I saw was in a swampy area. Jerry had sent me to this area because of all the deer tracks that he had seen there the day before. As I was walking through it, a small bull moose came walking out of the trees and down into the swamp towards me. I stood still while he looked at me, then he walked a little closer and began to demolish a small pine tree with his horns. I got the message and left the vicinity as fast as I could.

About a week and a half into the season, we were driving thru an area that had a large brush covered hill to our right. We spotted a large bull, bedded down about 300 yards up the hill laying in about 14-16 inches of snow. They are pretty easy to spot because their hair is almost jet black. Against the snow background, there is quite a contrast.

We stopped, got out of the truck and Jerry took a rest, and with one shot from his 30.06, the hunt was over. We put our pack boards on and crossed over a creek about 10 feet wide and then on up the steep hill. Jerry started butchering and I started packing. The first pack was the worst, which was because I brought the head and guns out first. With both rifles (one over each shoulder) and that large, heavy, unwieldy head it was a real chore.

I continued up and down that hill about six or seven more times until the meat was all down to the truck. Jerry helped me pack, but only about 30 lbs. that last trip. He had some excuse about his recent knee operation. I am going to remember that excuse if I ever need it. It worked for him and maybe it will work for me.

My partner Bill and I continue to put in for one of those special Washington draw tags every year, but so far have not been lucky enough to get one.

1995 Koyukuk River, Alaska - All horns over 50 inches wide.
(standing left to right) Lauren, Mike and Felix. (kneeling left to right)
Lauretta, Don and Sam. My horns are on the far left.

Lake Becharof, Alaska 1993 - My moose.
(Left to right) Myself, Sam, Bill, Don and Mike

CHAPTER 9
YEAR of the FOX

Maybe 10 years ago, I was deer hunting with one of my friends, John Stacy. We drove up to a place called Corral Pass, near Crystal Mountain, a popular skiing area in the Western Cascade Mountains of Washington. I had been introduced to this spot by another one of my friends, Mike Hudson, a year or so prior to this, when bear hunting.

The camping spot is a state camp ground with picnic tables, fire pits, and very clean out houses, if you can believe it. It is quite popular with mountain bikers, hikers and horse people. There are many miles of well-maintained trails with exquisite views of Mt Rainer and Mt Adams.

During my several hunts and camping trips there, I have seen mostly elk (including an albino cow), a few deer, mountain goats almost every time, and several bears on one trip. Anyway, we arrived about noon, set up camp and then did a short recon hunt and hike to show John a little of the area.

Mike had been hunting in the area a few days before John and I left on our trip and he said that he had seen a small spike in a spot he described to me. Obviously, the spike buck wasn't big enough for him, so he passed on it. His requirements are obviously higher than mine, any buck with a 1- inch horn is fair game for me.

About 20 to 25 years ago, I passed on a big spike on opening day and hunted the rest of the season without seeing another buck until close to the last day and had to settle for a small (barely legal) spike, much smaller than the one I passed on. I learned my lesson. Anyway, John and I got up the very next morning and left camp in different directions. John went East towards Crystal Mountain; I went West towards the area that Mike had seen the spike several days earlier.

After hunting most of the day, I started back to camp on one of the main hiking trails. Lo and behold, I spotted the spike and a doe feeding within about 25-30 feet off the trail I was on, and only about 100-150 feet away. Neither the buck nor doe seemed very spooked by my presence. I suppose they were somewhat used to all the hikers and bikers in the area. It only took me about 1 second to realize that I was looking at my years supply of venison. Tame deer or not, it would be just as tasty.

After gutting and skinning the deer, I packed the heart, liver, and head back to camp, arriving just about dark. John returned shortly and we exchanged stories about our day. He had not seen any deer, but said that he had seen what might have been a white horse running through the trees. I knew right away that what he had spotted was probably the blond side of a bull elk running away from him, or possibly that albino cow I had seen earlier. We actually spotted several bulls later on in the same area.

John is an Oklahoma boy and had not had much experience with elk at that time, so he did not know that most bulls are quite tan or blond looking and can be mistaken for something else, a horse in this case.

Well, I told him that he had probably spotted a bull elk from how he described it to me. He accepted that, and then realized that what he had seen was an elk, not a horse. Since then John has been on quite a few elk hunts and now can give me lessons on things I'm lacking.

After telling me about his "horse" experience, he asked me about my day. I said something or other and told him to go and look beside the tent. He did, and discovered the deer head. Of course, he chided me about not telling him from the get go, but we had a good laugh. That is the best part of any hunting, fishing or hiking trip is the enjoyment of being with good friends whom you can trust and have fun with.

Well anyway, we started a campfire, had dinner and a beer and went to bed. The next morning, we got up and prepared to go and pack out my deer. During the course of breakfast, getting the meat sheets and packs together, I happened to check on the deer head – it was gone!

We couldn't figure it out – where did it go?

Did someone come along during the night and steal it? or did some animal carry it off?

We looked all around the camp and adjacent area and finally found the tag which had been ripped off it's ear, about 75-100 feet from the tent. We also found some fresh scat that might have come from what we thought might be coyote or bob cat. We finally gave up on finding the head and left to retrieve the meat, all the time wondering what a game warden would say if he happened by. Possessing a deer without proof of sex is not a good thing.

We boned out the rib cage and cut off the legs and loaded our pack boards. One of us had both hind quarters and the other had the 2 front legs, backstraps and rib and burger meat. I also retrieved the private parts, and placed them in a zip lock bag, for proof that it was a buck, since we did not have a head anymore.

We got back to camp and put what we could in the cooler and hung up the legs. John then went back out hunting and I decided to start boning out the legs. I was quite nervous about a game warden coming around, especially since we were in a state camp ground. There weren't any other hunters camped there, but since I butcher my own game anyway, I decided to start the boning out process then and there.

I had one of the front legs finished and was starting on the other, when I looked up from the picnic table I was using, which was just across the road from our camp, and lo and behold, there stood a fox in the middle of the road, about 40 ft away, staring at me. He or she was a beautiful silver colored fox with a black tail. I have seen several red foxes in the wild, but never before or after a silver one.

It just stood there staring at me as if asking for a piece of my deer. I then realized, he was the ornery thief that had run off with my deer head the previous night. The fox had probably gotten used to scavenging whatever he could from all the careless campers in the area. Since the deer head was only a spike, he was able to pack it off to his den. I then threw him one of the boned-out legs, and he immediately grabbed it and headed off uphill into the woods.

After he was gone, I continued boning out another leg. In about 30 or 40 minutes, he returned for another hand out. I got the bright idea that if I threw him another bigger bone, he would grab it and head for his den again. I thought if I was fast enough, I might be able to follow him to his den and retrieve my deer head. Very foolish on my part. I threw him a big bone and off he went. I ran after him as fast as I could, and lost sight of him after about 200 feet. What on earth was I thinking of, to think I could keep up with a fox. That was the last I saw of him and obviously, I never found the head.

John was not successful that day or the next morning, and so we left for home with a buck deer, but no real proof that it was antlered. We can laugh about it now, but still wonder what a game warden would have said or done if we had been discovered.

Another lesson in hunting, protect not only your game meat, but the proof of a legal kill as well. Another lesson, never trust a fox (woman or animal).

A gorgeous silver fox. Although gorgeous, it was a thief.

CHAPTER 10

YEAR of the DOG

The 2011 elk season started out on a bitter sweet note. The bitter far outweighed the sweet. The sweet was that I had drawn a "any bull" tag which is a very coveted treat. The bitter was three other things. The first was that our longtime hunting partner, Jim Eagleton, was diagnosed with 4th stage lung cancer. The second was, that this was the 2nd year that our other partner Bob Wilson, would not be with us. He had retired and moved to Montana. The 3rd was, that Craig Harmeling from the Vashon Island camp had been bucked off his mule and broken his shoulder, and so would not be able to handle the rigors of setting up and taking down his camp. Also, his longtime hunting partner, Bob Stougaard was experiencing some health issues. This would be the first year in as long as I can remember (back to the 1950s) that the Vashon Island camp would not be hunting in the area we hunt.

Our three camps, the Whitehouse camp, the Vashon camp, and our camp have camped and hunted in the same area since the 1950s. Even though we are three separate camps, we operate as if we were partners. We have always had a great relationship with these other camps.

If any of us ever drives down to town for any supplies or whatever, we always check with the other camps to see if they might want us to pick something up. If one of the camps need any help such as special tools, cutting firewood, tent repair, packing game out, or actually anything, we all try to help out. I actually borrowed a rifle from the Vashon camp a couple of years ago because I had broken the stock on mine. We also all monitor the same channel on our radios.

For the past ten years or so we have all shared a midseason dinner, usually on Wed. night. Whoever hosts the dinner is responsible for the main course and the rest bring the hors d'oeuvre.

Believe me, these are no ordinary meals. Whoever hosts the dinner always seems to try and outdo the previous one. The worst dinner we ever had was just simply wonderful.

Our camp hosted the dinner the last year Bob hunted with us (2009). Our main course was fresh lobster to the tune of about 250 bucks for those clawed critters. At these dinners we almost always have smoked salmon, barbecued salmon or halibut, buttered shrimp, baked potatoes, salad, beanie weenies, and fresh pie from Don's wonderful wife, Ethel., all washed down with a plentiful variety of drinks. There is always a plentiful supply of stories, chatter, or BS. Most of these stories we have shared many times, but we usually still get a good laugh unless you might be the goat of the story. Most are somewhat true. The good times and sometimes even the bad times are what a hunting camp is all about. The memories are priceless. Ones partners are what really makes for a successful and enjoyable hunt. If we are blessed with a deer, elk, or whatever, then that is just icing on the cake.

Well anyway, since I drew a "any bull" tag, I had the privilege of being allowed to hunt five days prior to general modern firearms season and then another nine days of regular bull season, which gave me 14 days to harvest a bull.

This has always been ample time to do the deed. I had been drawn three other times prior to this season and had been successful in shooting two 5 points and a very nice 6 point, so felt quite confident in being successful this year also.

Jim is strictly a meat hunter, whereas Bill and I go for a big rack when we have been drawn for a "any bull" tag. Jim would whack a spike without hesitation even if he had one of these special tags. He tends to be a lot smarter than either Bill or myself. It is understood in no uncertain terms that if either Bill or myself shot a spike and wasted one of these prize tags on it before the last day or two before seasons end, we would pay the price of being humiliated until we left this sweet earth.

So, as things went, I passed on a spike opening morning and another spike about three days later. I still had not seen a branched antlered bull going into the general season.

Bill got off one shot at a spike opening morning of general season. He hit it and followed a spotty blood trail on dry ground until he lost all trace of it. Shortly after he had given up on it, he heard a shot not too far distant and in the same general direction the spike was headed. He figured another hunter had finished off his bull. He was a little down on himself but he never gives up.

He was hunting in an area we call the lower tams at the time. This large hill is mostly treed with tamarack trees, hence the name tamarack hill. There is a gated off logging road that circles the hill about midway up the hill. The above section is called upper tams while of course the lower section is called the lower tams. The upper half is comprised of several large meadows and several large and small patches of trees. Some of the treed areas are so thick that very little vegetation grows beneath the trees and other areas are quite open. The lower tams are almost all treed but not as thick as some of the upper tams. There is quite a large amount of brush in the lower tams.

Bill has always enjoyed hunting the lower tams and has done fairly well there.

Well, since I was not being very successful in locating a big bull in the areas we would normally find one, such as up by elk cabin, Bethel ridge area, or down in the canyons below camp, I decided to hunt near where Bill hunts in the lower tams.

I was hunting in an area that I had seen elk on previous hunts not too far from where Bill had set up a blind, when I heard a shot somewhat close to where he was located. I started walking slowly toward where I thought he might be and had gone a couple hundred yards when I decided to sit down on a convenient log and have a candy bar. From where I was sitting, I had great visibility looking down and to my right for about 200 yards. To my left was a thick tree line only about 50 or 60 feet away. Straight ahead I could see about 150 feet through brush and branches.

I had just pulled out my candy bar and taken one bite when I saw a movement directly in front of me. I immediately saw the head and upper chest of a large bull walking directly towards me about 125 feet away. I could only see the lower section of his rack due to limbs and brush. What I saw was two large eye guards and the base of the horns which appeared to be very thick. I said to myself, "this is the one I've been waiting for". He was just walking along unaware that I was anywhere around. If he had continued walking straight at me or passed in front of me, it would have been a piece of cake, but you guessed it, he did neither. He decided to turn a little to his right and passed just on the other side of those blocking trees and brush. This all occurred in about 2 seconds and I had remained absolutely still so as not to scare him. He still had no idea that there was any danger around. At that time, he was probably only about 100 feet away but on the other side of the thick doghair trees.

I looked and saw a small opening in the tree line about 80 or so feet away and watched his upper antlers pass through. He was still just meandering along. I quickly looked and spotted another small opening maybe about 70 feet away that was a tiny bit larger than the previous one. That would be my only chance of seeing him again. I brought my rifle up and aimed at the opening. In about 3 or 4 seconds I saw his horns and a small part of his head start to pass through that opening. The limbs and brush hid the rest of his body. Since he was such a short distance away and I knew I would not be able to see him again because of the even thicker trees and brush behind me, I decided to aim at a spot where I figured his front shoulders would be just behind those limbs and such. I pulled the trigger firing only one shot.

Nothing ___ I mean nothing___ nothing happened___ no brush crashing___ no hoof beats___ no sound at all!

I didn't know what to think. Had I killed him instantly and he was just lying there? Usually when an elk is frightened and it takes off running you can hear it thudding and crashing for a longways.

There was no sound at all!

So, I got up and slowly worked my way over to where I expected to see him lying there. Nothing!

I walked around, up and down, back and forth, for several hundred yards in every direction. No blood, no hair, no tracks, no elk. I then called Bill on the radio and he worked his way up to where I was. I told him my tale of woe and he then searched around the entire area also. Nothing!

As near as I can figure, my bullet must have either not penetrated thru all those trees and brush or ricocheted off a limb. That old bull must have just kept on walking and wondered what all the noise was.

Well anyway, a couple days after that episode, I spotted another large bull in a canyon (Joe's Canyon) below our camp. He was a very respectable 5 or 6 point, but not as large as the one I had first shot at. If I had been close enough to this second bull, I would have gladly taken him. He was standing in a small clearing about 6 or 700 yards across the canyon from me. I watched him for about 10 minutes or so just feeding through that clearing and then into a large patch of thick woods.

I have shot both a bull and a cow in that exact clearing in past years but from a different location which we call the, "pine tree". It is about a 350- or 400-yard shot from that location. The "pine tree" is on a bluff that juts out into the upper part of this canyon.

This canyon is an excellent place to hunt if you're willing to pack everything out on your back. It is very steep, rocky and full of brush and trees.

The elk and deer when pressured from other areas seem to congregate in this and other nearby canyons because very few hunters are willing to take a chance of shooting an animal down in these remote canyons due to the hard pack out. Most others think we are darn fools to do what we do. But we have been quite successful in doing so and do not mind the difficult pack out considering the rewards of bringing a critter home for dinner.

Since I still had about 4 days of season left, I figured I had a great chance of seeing this second bull again, but I never did.

So, after seeing four legal bulls and taking one single shot, I ended up eating my tag. It tasted just horrible. It was brought to my attention several times that perhaps I was foolish for passing on the first two spikes, but you know what, it's OK. I've weighed the consequences. Would it be better to be thought foolish by several hunting buddies for not taking the spikes or face the harassment I would have received from my partner and friend, Bill, for what he would have called shooting a baby elk when a real hunter would only take a trophy with that million dollar tag. Knowing that I will hopefully have many more seasons of hunting with Bill, I believe I made the correct choice.

Well anyway about the dog.

During the middle of the regular season (Wed.) we invited Greg Barnett from the Whitehouse camp up to have dinner with us since Don had left to go back to work for a couple of days. When he drove into our camp which was after dark, and parked his truck, he got out and said "whose dog is that?" We didn't know what he was talking about until he pointed out the dog in the beam of his flashlight.

It was a smallish brown dog about 30 or 35 pounds with one brown eye and one blue eye. I believe he was some sort of heeler or what some call a cattle dog.

We tried to coax him to us but he would have nothing to do with us, so we let him be and proceeded with our dinner and our happy hour. After Greg left for his own camp, Bill and I went to bed.

As a side note, Jim had only hunted for about three days because of being so sick and had gone home, so only Bill and I were in camp.

Sometime around midnight, I kept hearing a scratching noise near my head but slightly below the cot. I thought it might be mice rummaging around the tent and was somewhat irritated. This kept me awake for a half hour or so until I finally reached my arm over the cot and started moving gear around in hopes of scaring the mouse. I then felt a large, warm, soft lump against the outside of the tent wall. It baffled me at first until I remembered about the dog. It was freezing outside and he was obviously snuggled up to the warm tent to try and obtain some heat. I was right.

I went outside the tent with my flashlight and discovered the dog laying down against the tent right about where my head would be if I was on my cot. He just laid there staring up at me. I got a small package of bear jerky and threw a few pieces toward him. He had the whole package devoured in just a couple of minutes, but would still not come close enough to touch. But it was enough for him to become less cautious of me.

It was below freezing outside, so I went back inside the tent, put another chunk of wood in the stove, left the door flap slightly open and got back in my warm sleeping bag.

It wasn't long before I could hear some sniffing and rustling around inside the tent. I flipped on my flashlight and sure enough that dog had ventured in and was laying by the stove. He probably figured he'd died and gone to doggy heaven.

Bill got up and poured him a bowl full of water, which he immediately drained. He had been extremely thirsty and hungry and now fed and watered and warm he must have felt awfully good.

We went back to bed and soon that dog came over to my cot and let me pet him. After a bit he lay down beside me and went to sleep.

We slept in that morning, and when we got up, we discovered we had a new best friend. That dog had overcome most of his shyness and was jumping and running all around us, wanting to play. We fed him the same food we were eating, bacon, eggs, and toast for breakfast and hamburgers or whatever for lunch. He must have figured for sure that he was in the promised land eating nothing but delicious human food and not that nasty dog food.

We were concerned for several reasons. First, where did he come from? Who were his owners? Were they looking for him? And secondly, we wanted to get out hunting, but he would follow us wherever we went.

So, it was decided that Bill would get back to hunting and I would put him in my truck and take him with me to try and resolve some of the above questions. I drove all the way down to the Oak Creek Feeding Station (about 14 miles), stopping and talking to everybody I came across asking if they might know anything about the dog. Nobody knew any concrete facts about him but several hunters had seen him walking up the road the previous day. At the feeding station, one of the helpers had seen him down there two days prior to this.

I left word and a note at the feeding station and with a forest service worker about this dog and where we were camped.

Nobody ever responded.

Well anyway, that afternoon we wanted to get out hunting but the dog, which we started calling, "Brown Dog" wouldn't stay in camp, and we didn't want him to be following us around when we were traipsing through the woods trying to be quiet. So, Bill decided to shut him inside his pickup. We put him in the truck and everything seemed fine, so we went out for the evening hunt.

When we returned at dark, everything was just hunky dory. He hadn't seemed to mind the truck captivity at all. So, we thought, life is good. We bantered back and forth about who would take Brown Dog home at seasons end or what we would do with him.

We both had dogs at home, in fact Bill had three of them, but neither of us wanted another, although we were both becoming quite attached to him.

We spent another night with Brown Dog and come the next morning, we headed out hunting again. Since the previous afternoons hunt with the dog shut in Bill's truck went so well, we decided, actually Bill decided to do it again. This is important to remember that it was Bill's idea, not mine.

When we left camp, Bill headed down to the Flattop and I ventured out to the Willows Ridge and down the opposite side of the canyon.

At about noon I returned to camp and immediately walked over to Bill's truck to let good old Brown Dog out of prison. I opened the door and two things happened. The first thing was, Brown Dog jumped out and took off running. The second thing was that my pants almost turned the same color as our lovely dog.

I was stunned, shocked, amazed, and a few other unmentionable things. The inside of his immaculate truck was no longer immaculate. I really don't think a grenade could have caused much more damage. The whole headliner and the insulation looked as if it had gone through a meat grinder. None of it was recognizable. Both the front and back dome lights were torn off and hanging down. The front upper dome council was laying on the dashboard and chewed up. The headrest was torn off the passenger seat and the whole back was torn off the seat itself. Both back seatbelts were chewed off and there were wires and other unrecognizable pieces strewn throughout the cab.

Things had not gone quite as well as the afternoon before. Brown Dog was pretty happy to be out of that truck and although he seemed a little nervous it didn't affect his appetite or playful mood.

I stood around awhile pondering what I should do. I thought about trying to clean up some of the debris but realized it would be a useless task. I actually doubted whether the truck would even start up.

I then thought about the dog's wellbeing. What would Bill do when he returned and saw the horrible damage. Bill is usually quite easy going, but I have witnessed his temper a couple of times. It isn't pretty. I thought about it a bit and figured even if our new best friend would be allowed to live, what would we do with him for the rest of the season. We couldn't leave him tied up and I certainly wasn't going to sacrifice my pickup. We had been discussing what to do with him at seasons end anyway, and had considered the Yakima County Humane Society for adoption.

So, I decided that now was the time for that to happen, before Bill returned to camp. I thought it might be safer for Brown Dog.

I called Bill on the radio and said that I had decided to take Brown

Dog to the humane society right away instead of waiting until later. There was a pause before he said, "Did Brown Dog scratch up my door panels a bit?" There was another pause on my end before I said "No, actually your door panels are in pretty good shape, but everything else is pretty much destroyed."

He made it back to camp in record time.

When he walked up to his truck and saw all the damage, all he could say was "Oh, my gosh" ----- several times.

Then he said something that showed his true character. He said "You know what, it's my own fault, I should have known better." Brown Dog got his reprieve, although only short lived. We both decided that taking him to the humane society was our only option. Which I did that same day.

I drove the 30 or so miles to the humane society with that dog sitting right next to me, with his head almost always laying against the side of mine. He was a very loving animal. Leaving him at the humane society was one of the hardest things I have ever done. It is absolutely amazing how quickly an animal can capture your heart. I still think of him often, wondering if he was ever adopted. The lady at the society said he was young and very healthy and had a great chance of being adopted. I hope so. They gave him a number and named him "Thor" and said I could check back in to check his status, but to this day I have not had the courage to do so.

Well anyway, Don and Greg came up to camp to check out the disaster, and took some pictures. Since we monitor the same radio channel, they had heard our sad tale of woe. Don sent the pictures to his son Brian on his smart phone and after talking about it, we all decided to throw $5 into the pot and each give a guess as to the dollar amount of damage to the truck.

The estimates ranged between $2,000 and $5,000. When season ended, Bill took the truck to a body shop for repairs. It took them about 2 months to complete the work and the actual cost was $2,800 and change.

Thank goodness his insurance paid all but his $100 deductible.

Believe it or not the insurance company said that this was not an extraordinary case, that it happens quite often.

Anyway, that year is what we call "the year of the dog". Another hunting experience and lesson ------ beware of dogs, especially cute, brown, and friendly ones.

CHAPTER 11

YEAR of the BLIZZARD

During the elk season of 1985, we experienced a blizzard, and did we have problems. But for the grace of God, we may have had a tragedy at camp. It all started out in such a good and very exciting way, and then all hades broke loose.

It was in the middle of elk season with just a trace of snow on the ground, patches here and there. Bob, Dennis Bell, Larry Kyle, (Bob's father in law) and myself woke up one morning to the sight of a few small snowflakes falling. This is usually an exciting event for us because of the fact that snow on the ground has a huge impact on encouraging the elk migration out of the higher Cascade Mountains above and to the west of us. If we get a foot or two of snow at our camp which is at 5000 feet of elevation, means there is a heck of a lot more in the mountains above us.

Since we are directly in line of one of the primary migratory routes from around the base of Mt. Rainier, if not the main one, this increases our chances of intersecting them on the way to the Oak Creek Feeding Station. The most used migratory trail passes within about 100 yards of our camp. Deep snow is a blessing to us. We have taken quite a few elk and deer right from camp. It sure beats packing them out of the canyon, where we get most of our game. It usually takes a day or two after a big snow for us to start seeing the results of the migration.

We did a morning hunt and then returned to camp for lunch. By then the snowflakes started getting larger and a bit more frequent. Up to that point the flakes were very small and lightly falling. There was maybe 2 to 3 inches of new snow at that point.

At lunch, Bob's brother Bill, showed up at camp in his jeep with a girlfriend. With the arrival of company, including a handsome young lady, coupled with a significant increase of snowfall, we put away the guns and started having a small party.

When Bill and his girlfriend left about dark, about a foot of snow had accumulated, and it began snowing even harder and the wind picked up significantly.

We found out days later that Bill and his sweetheart had a very tough time getting back to Ellensburg, where he lived. In normal weather it takes about 35 minutes to get down to Hwy. #12 from our camp and then about an hour or so to get to Ellensburg. It's a good thing he had 4-wheel drive and chains, and is a good driver. Even so, he didn't make it home until the next morning. Apparently, part of the highway was closed due to accidents and plowing taking place.

Right after Bill left, the wind and snow increased until it was a full-blown blizzard. We were so excited about the prospect of what good fortune we were having with all the new snow, and the knowledge that the elk would be in full migration.

We had another beer or two and maybe a bite of dinner, of which I don't remember. Then all of a sudden, Bob had the bright idea of walking up to the camp above, about 400 yards or so. That camp is what we call the "Jim Jim's camp", due to the fact that father and son camped there, both named Jim.

Bob wanted to continue the celebration with them. Huge mistake!

By that time, about a foot and a half of snow had accumulated with a lot more coming. He bundled up, grabbed a bottle of hooch, and headed out despite our feeble warnings.

As soon as he left, I looked outside of the tent and saw that you could only see about 10 feet in any direction and it was blacker than the ace of spades. I knew he was headed for trouble. I grabbed a Coleman lantern or two and placed them outside the tent in hopes that he might be able to see the glow reflecting off the snow upon his return.

There was absolutely no use in venturing out in that blizzard and having both of us in trouble. Footsteps would fill up in just a couple of minutes. The three of us still at camp were plenty worried and felt completely helpless about the situation.

There is a saying that the Good Lord takes care of the stupid, dumb, and ignorant, and you might add intoxicated, and in this case He did. It seemed like hours but in fact it was probably only about a half an hour, when Bob came busting through the tent door. His eyes were the size of saucers, his face very red and the look of terror was upon him. You cannot believe the feeling of relief we all felt upon the safe return of our buddy, unless you may have been through a similar experience.

When he had left camp, he had started in a direct line towards Jim-Jim's camp, but soon realized there was no way he could stay on a straight line in the conditions he was in, what with the inky blackness and swirling snow and wind like it was. The way to Jim-Jim's was a direct line north about 400 or more yards through a large meadow until you came to a small grove of trees, of which their camp was in the middle. To the west was an abrupt cliff falling off into a deep canyon and to the east was a very large treed area with a few small clearings and no other camps within several miles.

When he realized that he wasn't going to find Jim-Jim's, he turned back in his tracks, which soon vanished in the falling and drifting snow. He knew he was in trouble. He tried orienting himself as to the direction of the wind, but it was swirling and changing directions so much, that was not an option either. He continued on until eventually coming upon a thick treed area which he figured to be the area east of camp so he changed directions again heading mostly to the west toward camp. It was a very good thing that he hadn't panicked and kept his wits about him. It's also very good that Bob is both physically and mentally tough and by that time quite sober.

Eventually, thanks be to God, he spotted a small glow in the dark, which were the lanterns we had placed outside. He turned toward the light and stumbled into camp. He said that he was probably only about 30 or so feet from camp when he spotted the glow and could have possibly walked right on by without finding us.

We heard days later that there were 2 or 3 deaths in close proximity to our camp that same night. I believe those deaths were from asphyxiation due to closed up campers or trailers, but there could just as well been more due to the extreme cold, amount of snow, and zero visibility.

Well anyway, we eventually sacked out and when we awoke in the morning, snow had drifted into the tent, although it was zipped up pretty tight, except for the two small holes in the top at either end where the ridge pole and ropes pass through. When we opened the tent door flap, we discovered that we could not get out, due to about 5 feet of snow that had drifted against the tent.

By then the storm had passed, leaving about four feet of new snow. We have five-foot sidewalls on our tent, and it had drifted well over the top of those.

We had to claw and crawl our way out of the tent to get to the shovels which were stored in the outhouse. We then shoveled a path from the outhouse/storage shed to the tent and to the two 4-wheel drive vehicles. We had to shovel snow away from the doors before being able to open them, and around all the wheels to be able to install the chains. After chaining all four wheels of each vehicle, neither rig would move at all due to the vast amount of snow blocking the path in both directions. By then we knew we were in a heap of trouble.

We had to dig the snow away from the path of the vehicles to within one foot of the ground to get them to move at all. Eventually we got the vehicles turned around and headed in the right direction, and then dug a path about 50 feet long in front of the lead vehicle, so we could get a run at the deeper snow. We thought that if we could build up a little speed, we might be able to plow our way through. WRONG!

After taking off as fast as we could go in the space of about 50 feet, we would hit the wall of snow and only penetrate about another 6 or 8 feet before coming to a complete stop with snow covering the hood and windshield.

We then had breakfast, had completely given up on hunting, and started digging.

Three of us started digging out the road while Larry, the old guy in camp, kept up the camp, digging out the tent, cooking and washing dishes, and keeping the fire going. We would dig about 75 to 100 feet of road and then drive forward as far as possible, and then dig some more. This continued all day with Larry keeping us supplied with food, sodas, and coffee.

Finally, young Jim made it down to our camp with his snowmobile. The snow was so deep and soft that his snowmobile was practically useless. He had to dig out a partial path for it to keep moving, although not as deep as for the vehicles. The snowmobile was practically no use to us until the last day in camp, when we hooked an old car hood to it to act as a sled, to ferry out all of both camps to the main forest service road about a mile away. We used the shoveled-out path we had dug for the vehicles. The forest service road had been cleared using a private bulldozer by the second evening after the storm. It took us three full days of digging well past dark, to make it to the main cleared road.

The first day, we got our trucks down to the Whitehouse camp, which is about one-third of a mile from us. It just so happened that they were not elk hunting that year, so the camp was vacant. Our primary concern was to get our rigs out before another storm set in. If we could get our trucks down to the main road, we figured we could use the snowmobile to get the camps out and down to the trucks if another batch of snow hit us.

In the meantime, young Jim was digging a road down to our camp, at which time he could use our cleared road to get the rest of the way out.

Towards the end of the first day when we were digging past the Whitehouse camp, we discovered a 2-wheel drive pickup stuck in a meadow about 250 feet away from our dugout road. There were three men just sitting in it seemingly doing nothing to get out. They had no chains or shovel and no means of heat, except for the truck heater, which they were using sparingly. Their only food was a couple of frozen tortillas. They had apparently driven up for a day hunt, gotten stuck in the blizzard and ended up not getting out until the third day like we did.

All three of them walked back to camp with us. We fed them and offered our warm tent for the night. The two younger men chose to walk back to their cold pickup and spend the night, but the older gentleman chose to stay with us in the toasty warm tent. He had been near hypothermic when we came across them and seemed very grateful for our assistance. It was a bit difficult conversing with them since only one of them spoke a tiny bit of English. Our languages were different but we were able to communicate in an OK manner. As it turned out the older fellow spent the rest of time in our camp with Larry until we all were able to get out.

The second day of digging proved to be quite eventful. We got up and started digging before light and stuck with it until midnight or so. In the meantime, we had loaned a shovel to the two stranded younger men, so they could dig a road that would intersect our cleared one.

Sometime before noon an army helicopter with a Yakima County deputy sheriff landed at Jim-Jim's camp and then flew down to where we were digging. The deputy got out and informed us we had five minutes to make up our minds if we wanted to get a ride out on the chopper, leaving our entire camp behind, including our rifles, or stay and suffer the consequences if another storm set in leaving us stranded even longer. He said there was a chance they would not return if we chose to stay. I realize that they had a large area to cover and were strapped for time, but we all thought he could have been a little friendlier or more diplomatic about it. Our camp was all of the same accord that there was not much of a choice. We were not going to leave everything to the winter elements or thieves.

We chose to stay and dig our guts out. Although, old Jim from the above camp, chose to fly out to comfort in a nice motel until young Jim could finally get out.

We thought that old Jim, once he was back to civilization, would find some sort of way to help us out of our predicament, but we never saw nor heard from him again until next hunting season. Well anyway, Larry kept us supplied with drink and food while we kept on digging for the rest of day two. We dug until after dark and got about another third of a mile of road cleared, then walked back to camp.

That night, a man showed up at camp just after dark on a snowmobile. He said, he had been hired by other hunters camped on the main road to bulldoze the road to their camps. He wanted another four or five hundred dollars from us to clear the last tenth of a mile of our access road, and that we should pay more for our share of the main road he had already cleared. We still had not even seen the main road or talked to any other hunters to verify his story. We didn't know if he was legit or not or just after some easy money. Things just didn't seem right. We talked it over and scraped up 80 or 90 bucks for our share of the main road and sent him on his way. Because our trucks were so far away from camp and because of that strange man, Dennis grabbed his sleeping bag and a sidearm and walked down to the trucks, and spent the night there.

On day three, we were digging before light and finished our side road that connected to the main road sometime after dark. That evening we had no idea where the bulldozer man was or what had become of him, except that the main road had been cleared.

At the end of that third day, Bob and young Jim drove to Yakima and procured an old car hood from a wrecking yard and brought it back to camp so we could attach it to Jim's snowmobile with ropes, and sled our camps out. Dennis spent another night alone in his pickup down by the main road. The three men in the stranded truck made it out that night and went on their way.

The last night in camp, there was just Larry and I, since Dennis was down in his truck and Bob was in Yakima with young Jim, when the strangest thing happened. About 1 A.M., Larry and I were abruptly woken up with the tent shaking so badly we thought it might come down. There was no wind at all and no sound, either. What could it be? We were both badly shaken; I won't say scared, although we may have been that too. We grabbed our guns and sat up for an hour or so until exhaustion set in and we went back to sleep.

Upon getting up in the morning, we realized what had happened the night before. A large elk herd had passed right through our camp. We had at that time, a large rope that passed through the top ridge of the tent and was attached to a tree about 20 feet away. The rope was about seven feet above the ground where it was attached to the tent and about ten feet above ground where it was attached to the tree. With the depth of the snow, the line was considerably lower to the ground than normal. Apparently, a tall antlered bull had got his horns tangled in the rope on his way through camp and had been shaking the tent to get untangled. On that fourth day we transferred all our tents and gear by car hood down to our trucks and got out of Dodge. We heard later that the lowland hunters that stuck it out to the end of season did very well, and that the elk were in full migration. By the end of that fourth day we were cold, wet, and exhausted. We wanted nothing more than to be home where there was a warm, dry, clean, bed with our lovely wives waiting.

CHAPTER 12

YEAR of the HELICOPTER

As far as hunting goes, the year of 2002, started out on a sour note for me, but for Bob and Bill, it started out great. Then during deer season, disaster struck Bill, also. Bob, on the other hand, continued having a stellar year. Let me explain. Sometime during early summer, I was attending a men's weekend retreat and somehow got talked into participating in a basketball game. This was a very foolish thing to do for a man sixty years old.

I was moving around pretty good, and way more involved than I should have been. At one point, I attempted a jump-shot, and to my surprise, it felt like someone had stepped on my right heel. I immediately dropped to the floor and looked around to see who the culprit was. Nobody was close enough to have done the deed.

The area around my ankle hurt a little bit, but not too bad. I stood up, but found walking was quite difficult. My foot did not function like it should; it kind of flopped around. It only took a second or two, to figure out that my basketball game was finished. The whole episode was somewhat confusing. I still couldn't figure out what damage had been done to my ankle or foot. I still didn't know which it was, ankle or foot.

Well anyway, I drove home the next day, but had trouble using the gas pedal. Everybody I know uses their right foot for both the gas and brake pedals, but I had to use my left foot. It was very awkward and confusing, but I somehow managed to get home without causing a wreck or any other disaster.

I went to the doctor Monday, and found out that I had severed my Achilles tendon. I used a splint and crutches for a couple days until an orthopedic surgeon did his magic on me. He sewed the two ends together and put on an adjustable splint, which I had to wear for several months. As I recall, I was allowed to put weight on the leg right away, but had to continue using the crutches. The good thing about using an adjustable splint instead of a solid cast, was that the doctor was able to adjust the movement of the leg as the tendon healed, so when it was time for physical therapy, the tendon had already been stretched to where it should be. That saved a lot of pain and therapy time later.

After about three months, I was able to shed the splint and get on with the physical therapy, which lasted a couple of months. I had just finished with the therapy when deer season started. The doctor severely warned me to not even think about any steep up or down hill walking or any brush busting. Those orders really put a crimp in my style of hunting. I was limited to camp maintenance, and a lot of sitting or standing around camp, waiting for some horned critter to wander by. That was not ideal, but at least I was there.

Bob and Bill were hunting the canyons. Jim mostly hunted in his blind, up towards Bethel Ridge, and Dorn (Bill's father-in-law), hunted the flats and the springs, near camp.

After about three days of this, I was bored stiff. I talked Bill into letting me walk down and out to the flattop, to his favorite spot which we call "the point". The "point" is a rock bluff that overlooks Joe's Canyon. This point is a great spot to sit and view a huge area of shale slides, treed areas, and several large clearings. We have harvested quite a few deer and several elk from that spot. Since this was his favorite blind, it was very kind of him to let me hunt there. We all have our special or favorite places to hunt, which the rest of the group respects and try to stay away from.

He then decided to drop down into the canyon below the "point" and continue further down and out Joe's Ridge. This is a very steep and rugged area.

Big mistake!

I walked very slowly and carefully out to the Flattop and set up on the "point", at first light. After sitting there for an hour or so, I saw Bill pass through the shale about 500 yards below me. He continued on until disappearing into the trees on my right.

About ten or fifteen minutes later, I heard this horrible scream on the two-way radio, and then Bill transmitting something about possibly breaking his leg. He had been side-hilling along a steep and slippery section, when he either slipped, a rock rolled under his boot, or something else happened to cause him to lurch downhill. He felt a sudden serious pain in his thigh, that caused him to fall to the ground. He laid there awhile, until the initial pain subsided and then attempted to stand, but found this an impossible task.

It was a very good thing that we all had radios.

When Bob heard what happened, he beat feet as fast as he could out of the Willows Canyon, up Willows Ridge, down the same ridge into Joe's Canyon and then up the other side of the canyon to where Bill was laying. That took him a little over a half hour, which was really smoking. All this time I was standing on the "point", feeling completely useless. I was the closest to Bill, but could do nothing but pass on information over the radio. I could not get down to where he was laying, or get back out of that hole, because of my healing Achilles tendon. If I would have attempted to have gone down to where he was, there would have been two of us to rescue instead of just one.

Since Dorn was in camp and heard everything that was happening, he called 911 on his cell phone. He got ahold of Yakima County dispatch, who in turn sent an ambulance up to our camp. When the ambulance arrived, the medics were in no-way going down into that canyon to retrieve Bill. The nearby army base was then notified, knowing that they had several helicopter crews who were anxious for the rescue which would be beneficial for their training. Thank goodness for our soldiers. After another half hour or so, we could see and hear a chopper coming up the White Pass highway towards us. When it reached our canyon, it veered up towards us. At first it went on by, but soon came back to hover directly over our injured compatriot. After a bit, a corpsman was lowered down to the ground. He did a quick analysis, and then a basket was purged out of the chopper and lowered to the ground, also. While the corpsman stabilized Bill and tucked him into his nice little comfy basket, the chopper flew up to our camp and set down for a bit. When all was ready, the chopper flew back out and down to Bill and his new friend. They were both winched up to, and into the chopper and away they flew. They went directly to the Yakima County Hospital. Bill was inspected thoroughly, and it was determined that he had torn one of the large muscle groups from his thigh. He was operated on the next day and sent home the day after. It was very obvious that his hunting was over for the year. As I mentioned at the beginning of this chapter, this had started out to be a great year for both Bob and Bill, due to the fact that both had drawn an "any bull" tag. This was a wonderful and rare event for elk hunters in our hunting area.

I recall Bill saying something like, "The worst part of this whole fiasco was that he would not be able to go elk hunting, and would lose that coveted tag." That part was worse than the fact of being casted for a long time.

I have to mention the fact that Bill, knowing that I had broken my tendon while playing basketball, had erected a hoop on a tree in camp, with a basketball sitting underneath, prior to my arrival to camp. He thought that was pretty funny.

Paybacks are sweet!

Since we knew that Pam would bring Bill up to camp on break-down day to retrieve his gear and junk, we went to town and bought a toy battery powered helicopter, complete with flashing light and blades that whirled around. When he crutched himself into the tent, on break-down day, the activated chopper was hanging directly in front of him.

I love paybacks!

As I mentioned earlier, Bob had a great season. Using his special tag, he bagged the largest elk of his life (so far). It was a huge 6X6, shot from what we call Elk Rock.

As a side note, Bill contacted the game department about his accident. As a result, he wasn't able to use his special tag that year, but didn't lose his lottery points. As a result of that, he was lucky enough to draw another "any bull" tag the next year, and shot a huge 6X6 off of the same Elk Rock that Bob had gotten his, the year before.

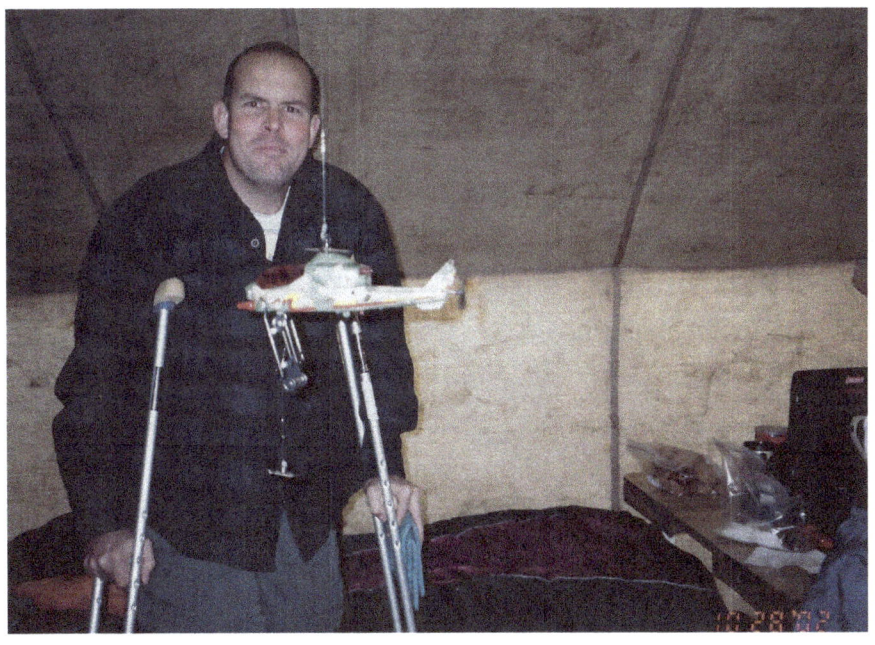

Breakdown day 2002 - Bill on crutches, upset with us about the toy helicopter. Paybacks are fun.

CHAPTER 13

RARE PHENOMENA and BEAUTY

THE BROCKEN SPECTER

Every so often things or events happen that seem unexplainable in one's life. This was one of those events for me.

Several years ago, I was elk hunting in the Oak Creek area and decided to hunt in what we call the Red Rock Canyon. This is the canyon between what we call the Hell Hole Ridge and the Red Rock Ridge.

I left camp before light and walked about a mile to where I could sneak out on a rock outcropping where I could sit and have a great view of both side ridges and the canyon below me. If you can get there before it gets too light, you have a great chance of spotting game, either feeding or on their way to a bedding area. Also, it is a wonderful place to be rewarded by the warmth of the rising sun which comes from the southeast over the top of the distant mountains in that direction.

On this particular day, it had been foggy and damp from the night before. When the sun rose, I stood up to catch the warmth from its rays and also to get a better view of the canyon below me. The fog was rising out of the canyon, and as I stood up with the sun on my left, I glanced out and over to my right. When I did that, I was astounded, amazed, startled, and a little apprehensive at what I saw.

About 100 to 150 yards away was another large rock outcropping that had somewhat of a flat surface that faced towards me. On that rock face was a human looking figure about 10-12 feet tall completely encircled by a completely round rainbow, and the whole image and rainbow was itself completely surrounded by a dazzling bright white fog.

I didn't know what to think about it. Was it a supernatural being? Was I experiencing the second coming? Was I in danger, or being blessed? I couldn't figure out what I was looking at. It was actually kind of unnerving and spooky.

After watching that phenomena for several minutes, I finally moved my arms a bit and noticed the huge image did the same. That was when I realized I was observing my own shadow being broadcast upon that other rock face. The whole experienced lasted about 8 or 10 minutes before it all faded away.

It was one of the strangest experiences of my life. I couldn't figure out what I had observed or how it all happened until I remembered that the sun was on the opposite side of me henceforth causing the shadow, but what caused the rainbow to completely encircle the human like form and all surrounded by the brilliant white fog. It all was beyond my understanding. It looked very similar to the pictures you see of Jesus with a halo surrounding his head, but this rainbow surrounded the whole body. Several years later, I was reading a book that told of this same experience that occurred in a dormant volcano on the island of Maui, Hawaii. When I read the story, it dawned on me that it was the exact same phenomena which I had experienced. There is a name for this event. It is called "The Brocken Specter" and was first experienced and recorded and given its name by someone who experienced it on Brocken Mountain in Germany. I know of no one else in my circle of family and friends who have observed that rare phenomena. I truly wished that I had taken a picture of it.

WHITE DIAMONDS

I believe it was the elk season of either 2009 or 2010. I again was hunting in the Oak Creek area out of our regular camp.

On that particular day, I had left camp in the morning and had walked past the Whitehouse camp and on over to and down what we call the Willows Ridge. I hunted down the ridge to what we call

Elk Rock. Bob, Bill, and I have all shot 6X6 bulls from that very rock, hence the name.

After hunting from the rock for several hours, and slowly hunting back up the ridge, I came to a steep meadow that is about 100 yards long. The sun had just peeked through the cloud layer and even though the temperature was hovering around 30 degrees, I became quite warm and was a little tired from the steep climb out of the canyon. Just a little-way from the top of the meadow, I made the decision to stop and lay down in the soft grass with the warm sun on my tired old body. What a perfect place to still hunt for a short spell. Sometimes these short still hunts in the sun turn into eye closing experiences, if you know what I mean. There are some who call them naps.

When I laid down in the bright warm sun, it soon started snowing. Not just regular snow but huge flakes. The cloud from which the snow came was quite a way off to my left side. The wind must have blown the snow out from under that cloud towards me. The sun was still shining on me and just as warm, but the snow was falling heavily and with huge flakes. That seemed very bizarre to me, to be laying in the sun as warm as can be and being snowed on.

But the strangest thing was that each flake appeared to look like a huge white diamond falling from the sky. I suppose the sun was reflecting off of each flake causing them to sparkle like diamonds. It was the most beautiful snowfall I have ever witnessed. I just lay there transfixed, enjoying the experience for about 10 minutes until it stopped snowing.

What a great experience I was blessed with. Most hunters, fishermen, and other outdoors people have witnessed similar and other wonderful phenomena such as the two I have described in this chapter.

CHAPTER 14

MY WORST and MOST EMBARRASSING HUNTS

The title of this book is "Adventures and Confessions of a Hunter". Well, this is the confession segment. I might add that I am not happy at all, or excited about fessing up to these horrible stories, but, am compelled to do so. I was taught to own up to my mistakes, so please don't judge me too harshly. Here are three stories that I am totally ashamed of myself and embarrassed about. They never should have happened.

Almost every hunter that I know well, has committed at least one mistake if not more while hunting. This fact is no excuse for me and does not make what I did OK. It is just a comment and food for thought. We are all responsible for our own actions.

I've committed a number of embarrassing errors, but am only going to tell you about what I consider the three worst ones. Two were while elk hunting and the other was while I was deer hunting. All three occurred while I was hunting out of our Oak Creek camp.

The deer episode occurred about 10 years ago, towards the end of the season. In Eastern Washington, we only get one week of modern firearm deer season. We used to get two weeks and allowed to shoot any buck with at least a one- inch horn. Then through the wisdom of our Washington wildlife commission the season was shortened to one week and a three- point minimum restriction was established.

Before these changes were made, our camp and the other nearby camps, were very successful in bagging a buck almost every year.

Now the success ratio is a buck every three or four years and the mature bucks we expected are just not there.

Another problem is, the second week we lost, was closer to the times of migration from the higher mountains to the west of us. It is amazing to witness the difference a week or two makes concerning the amount of game we see in our hunting area.

Since the rule changes, the number of deer camps have dwindled significantly. There is much frustration directed towards the game department. I thought the game dept. was trying to encourage more hunters, but instead, it is my opinion they are discouraging and losing more of them. It is difficult to encourage young hunters to get involved when the amount of game has dwindled so significantly. Sometimes, this frustration has a detrimental effect on our thoughts, attitudes, and actions. Anyway, back to my horrible deer experience. I had missed an easy shot at a nice buck the afternoon before this bad thing happened, so, was already a little frustrated. Since the rule changes I mentioned in the above paragraphs, if you were blessed with seeing a legal buck, you had better make it count, because the chances of seeing another were pretty slim.

We always get up very early, have breakfast, and are usually out of camp well before sunup, which I did this particular morning. I was walking towards the Whitehouse camp, maybe 15 or 20 minutes before legal shooting time and it was just getting a little light. All of a sudden, I heard the unmistakable thumping of a running and hopping deer. I glanced to my right and saw a doe and a nice buck with legal horns, running alongside me at about 75 feet away. It was light enough to see the rack and determine there was a safe background for a shot. They were clearly outlined against the early morning sky. Without hesitation, I raised my rifle, centered the buck in my scope and fired. He dropped like a ton of bricks. This all occurred in about three seconds. The time of day had not even entered my tiny little mind, until after it was over. It was a knee jerk reaction of which I am not proud of, but it happened. I drug the buck to camp which was only about 150 yards and butchered him right there.

As a result of this event, I have been dubbed the "night shooter" by my buddies, in particular the no goods from the Whitehouse camp.

The second mistake I will confess to, was also while hunting out of our Oak Creek camp, about 15 years ago. It was in the middle of elk season and we were lucky enough to have about a foot or more of snow. Bob was out on the Flattop below camp, Bill was down the Willows ridge on the flattop side of that ridge, and I was down the Willows ridge on the Red Rock side of that ridge. I had been watching two cows feeding in and out of some trees across the canyon, just below the Red Rock ridge for several hours. They were about 700 yards away from me. I dropped down about 150 yards further into the canyon to get a closer look at them, when I spotted a third elk. I glassed him and saw that he was a spike. He was the only legal bull I had seen all season so was quite excited. It was already afternoon, so figured I had best take the shot before it got too late. I shoot a 300 Win. Mag., which was plenty of gun for the 550 to 600-yard shot. I had never taken this long of a shot or done so since, but was willing to give it a go.

I laid down, got a solid rest and raised the cross-hairs about a foot or so above his shoulders and squeezed one off. When I steadied the rifle after the recoil, I saw that all three elk had disappeared.

I knew I had no choice but to make my way down through the canyon and up the other side to see if I had hit him. This is a cardinal rule in our camp, "if you take a shot at game, you had best be willing to go see if you hit him or not, no matter the distance or time it takes". No Exceptions!

It took me probably 45 minutes or longer to walk down through that brush and snow to get close to where they had been standing. I was within about 75 yards and just below where they had been feeding, and was walking up to that spot, when two cows stood up, directly above me about 25 yards away. I said to myself "Well, there are the two cows, now where is the spike?" Just then, the spike stood up about 100 feet away and stood there a bit too long. I pulled up my rifle and dropped him right there.

I quickly notched my tag, gutted and skinned him. I placed the heart and liver in my game bag, grabbed the head and started out of that steep and deep canyon. I did not get back to camp until an hour or so past dark. It was a long, but satisfying day. When I got back to camp, I found out that Bill had also shot a spike in Joe's Canyon at the same time I had taken my first shot in the Willows Canyon. When Bill and I were both shooting at the same time in different canyons, Bob was saying to himself "Here I am just sitting here, while my buddies are both killing elk." I think he was feeling a bit frustrated and useless, but we made him feel very useful the next two days packing out meat.

The next morning, we decided to pack my elk out first, since it was the farthest away and most difficult ground to climb out of. We grabbed our packs and hiked down the Red Rock Ridge, dropped off the ridge and on down to where my elk was laying. This is the embarrassing part.

When we got to within about 75 feet of where my bull was laying, Bill looked up the hill and said "That looks like an elk laying behind that log." I looked up hill but did not see anything, so thought he was pulling my leg. He then pointed out a leg sticking out above the log. How he spotted that, I still don't know, but sure enough when I walked uphill about 75 feet or so, there was a spike lying dead just on the other side of that log. I was completely shocked. Apparently, when I had taken the first shot across the canyon, which was well over 500 yards, the bullet had hit him right where I had aimed. It must have dropped him on the spot and he had slid down the steep and snowy slope and up against the back side of that log.

Since I had been watching two cows and one spike, which I had first shot at, I figured the two cows and one spike I came across just below where the first three were, had to have been the same three. How wrong I was!

If I hadn't seen and dropped that second spike, I would have walked right up to where the first one was laying. I had tried doing the right thing but was foiled by the confusion of seeing and shooting the second spike, which I was sure was the original one.

Since it was laying in snow and had apparently bled out, I had hopes of salvaging that one also. Bob still had his tag, so would have tagged it if the meat was still good. I saw that it had already bloated quite badly, but still attempted to gut it. When I started to slit the belly open to gut it, it literally exploded, spraying this nasty stuff all over the place. It had already spoiled beyond salvaging. What a waste.

The lesson being; even though I was sure the second bull was the same one I first shot at, I should have walked another 100 feet or more up that hill anyway, just to make sure.

My third mistake was the worst. This happened about 20 years ago.

Jim, Bob, Bill, and I were elk hunting out of the Oak Creek camp on opening morning. Bob, Bill, and I walked up towards Bethel Ridge and got as far as an area we call "the shooting gallery" just a few minutes before legal shooting time. This is a very large meadow that is between two large stands of trees. The hunters camped on Bethel Ridge walk out and down to it from the north and we walk up to it from the south. There are usually several bulls taken out of this meadow every season, hence the name. As we approached the meadow, we pushed out two spikes ahead of us in the semi darkness. For about five minutes or so, they just meandered around in that open meadow with probably eight or ten hunters watching them. They appeared to be very confused not knowing which way to go. Any direction they looked, they could more than likely see a hunter watching them. The three of us were the closest, but were unwilling to take a shot with so many witnesses, being that it was still about eight or ten minutes before legal shooting time. That fact obviously didn't bother two other hunters. First one was dropped, and then about ten seconds later the second one was shot.

Nobody moved.

We waited until a few minutes past legal shooting time and then walked right up to, and past both bulls. We then walked on up the hill past the two shooters, still in their blind, and entered the woods on the Bethel Ridge side of the meadow. I then looked back to watch the two fellows finally get out of their blind and start down towards the bulls. They were more than likely a little nervous about starting the season a little early.

We three talked it over, and came to the conclusion that we did the right thing, about not shooting early even though it cost us a couple of fine bulls.

We then split up going in three different directions. I chose to walk up and past the other hunters still on the north side of the meadow and enter the woods above them. I was cougaring along thru the trees and small clearings, when I spotted three elk running across a small clearing just in front of me, a cow, a calf, and a spike.

They were only about 150 feet away when I first spotted them. The cow and calf ran past a small grove of trees and stopped about 20 or so feet past the trees right in plain sight and only about 100 feet from me. The spike was right on their heels, but stopped just inside that small batch of trees. I could plainly see his whole body, including his front shoulders, but his head was hidden by several branches. I knew that it was the bull, but I wanted to see his head just to be 100% sure, instead of just 99% sure. I was trying to do it right.

I had raised my rifle to my shoulder, with his left shoulder in the middle of the scope, but still wouldn't squeeze off the shot until I saw his head. In the meantime, the cow was staring directly at me. All four of us just stood there motionless until after a couple of minutes, my arms got so tired, I had to lower the rifle a bit. As soon as I moved, that cow and calf vacated the area in record time with the spike right on their tail. Since he was still behind that little batch of trees, I could not get off a decent shot. By that time, I had seen three legal bulls and still had not squeezed the trigger. I was quite excited about seeing so much game, but a little exasperated about still not having anything to show for it. I then headed out in the general direction they had gone. After about 20 minutes or so, I busted another small group of elk, maybe six or seven head. Right away, I spotted another spike and was determined not to let this one get away. He was running right across in front of me, about 100 feet away headed for a batch of trees only a few feet in front of him. I took a quick shot at him just as he entered the thicket. He disappeared into the trees, but I knew that I had hit him.

I started running towards that grove of trees when he reversed his direction, or so I thought, and ran back directly in front of me, only about 50 feet away, headed for some other nearby trees. I instantly snapped off a quick shot at his blond body and he immediately disappeared in some thick woods.

As soon as I took that shot, I knew he wasn't the same elk. It immediately gave me a sick feeling. It was a very, very poor decision. I rarely swear, but I sure as hell wanted to.

I walked another 25 or 30 feet into the trees that the spike had run into, and there he stood, just getting ready to fall over. I finished him off, tagged, gutted, and skinned him.

I was very sure that I had hit the second elk also, so I followed his tracks and found him lying dead about 100 yards away. He was a bull calf, hence the blond hide. He also had short nubbins, but not enough to be classified as a legal bull. If he had been legal, one of my partners would have tagged him as I would have for them. I then proceeded to gut and skin him also, so as not to waste the meat.

I then returned to camp with the head and organs of the spike, and told my sad and embarrassing tale of woe. It ruined the joy of an otherwise successful day. None of us were pleased about the situation. They helped me pack out the legal bull, but I was on my own with the bull calf.

I went back to where it was, and boned it out completely. I then, by myself, packed it back to camp and stored it in my truck canopy. I was not about to waste the meat just because of my stupid mistake. If I had gotten caught, I would have taken full responsibility and paid my dues.

Some would say, I should have turned myself in and suffered the consequences. As in most fines levied against an offender, they are given to teach you a lesson not to do something again that is illegal, whether it is speeding, driving intoxicated, or shooting an illegal animal. I didn't need to pay out a thousand or more dollars just to reinforce a lesson that I had just learned big-time. I didn't want to compound the injury I had just experienced by paying out that amount of money, if I didn't have to.

I am for sure not saying that this was the correct thing to do, but I did it. My conscience has paid the price big time ever since. There are a number of things in my life that I wish I could do a "do over", and this is one of them.

A lesson: make sure of your target before pulling the trigger.

CHAPTER 15

FRIEND, GIRLFRIEND, BOYFRIEND

Being as this is a family friendly book, I will tell this story in the best manner I am able, without using some of the words that may or may not have been used in our elk camp or other hunting camps since.

On one very cold morning with about a foot and a half of snow on the ground, Bob and I decided to hike about a mile and a half up and over Bethel Ridge and down the other side into the Rattlesnake drainage. Neither of us had been that far down into that area before.

We got a very early start, well before light, hiked up and over the ridge and dropped down into the Rattlesnake just as it was breaking light. We separated and each went our separate way following a couple of well used animal trails. We never saw each other again until we were headed out of the canyon on our way up Bethel Ridge late in the afternoon. This was before we started carrying two-way radios. Because of what happened, I'm quite sure he would have contacted me right away and told me his interesting story much earlier.

After we separated that morning, I just meandered about for several hours following well used trails and seeing numerous fresh elk tracks. As I said earlier, it was well below freezing, so I had to keep moving to stay reasonably warm, which is the way I prefer to hunt anyway. I have a very difficult time staying in a blind for any length of time. I'm always wondering what is beyond the next group of trees or over the next hill. I have to admit that my way of hunting "walking" has been very beneficial to a number of other hunters who I have pushed game to, but that's OK.

After three or four hours without seeing another person or any animals, I encountered another hunter. He was a young man in his early 20's or so, and had a curious story he told me.

The first thing he asked me, was whether I had seen another guy who was with a girl. He went on to explain that he had traveled from an eastern state for this elk hunt with his girlfriend and his best friend. He was the only one actually hunting. Apparently, his girlfriend and buddy were just along for company, I guess.

I told him that I had not seen another person all morning, but if I ran across his friends, I would let them know he was looking for them. I thought it rather curious that they would separate in an unfamiliar area that none of them knew. We then said "good luck" and went our separate ways.

I hunted the rest of the day without seeing anything or anybody else, and then started back in the general direction of camp in the late afternoon. As it was, I wouldn't get back before dark.

On the way up the steep hill leading towards the top of Bethel Ridge, I heard somebody yell my name. I turned around, and there came Bob, beating feet up towards me. I could see his teeth at about 100 yards because of the huge smile on his face. When he caught up to me, he said, "Have I got a story for you". He then told me of his events of the day.

He had hunted all morning without seeing any game or another person, same as me. Sometime in the early afternoon, he found himself in a treed and brushy area sneaking along, when he heard some strange noises on the other side of some bushes and small trees. The noise sounded like some critter grunting or something similar. He couldn't imagine what the heck it was, so he sneaked around the edge of the bush. About 75 feet or so away was a large log laying in the snow, with a girl leaning over the log, and a guy standing directly behind her. Neither was dressed for the frigid weather, but neither seemed to mind. Actually, they were bare from their belly buttons to their knees. I will not describe what Bob told me they were doing, but I would imagine her boyfriend would not have been too pleased with the situation. Most best friends are willing to share almost anything, but not usually their girlfriends.

As cold as it was, we both wondered about the stamina of those two with so few clothes on.

One more story for future elk camps.

CHAPTER 16

USING HORSES — MY FIRST and LAST TIME

This story is about a deer hunting trip, using horses, with my friend, Ted Schmitz. Anybody who knows Ted, should know enough to never start, finish, or do anything in between with him. He has been one of my best friends since high school, and anytime I got in big trouble (including a couple of jail episodes) Ted was to blame. Well, he might see it the other way, but I know the truth. He is another one of my undeserving friends that wound up with a gorgeous and wonderful wife (Sandy), who for whatever reason has stayed with him for over 50 years. Talk about stamina.

Ted is one of those guys that can do just about anything, except stay out of trouble. He is an excellent mechanic, painter, machine operator, and has owned his own logging business for many years. He also owns several horses and mules, and he lives for hunting.

One time, many years ago, I let him talk me into going on a deer hunt in the Cascade Mountains using horses. It was the early deer hunt in the upper areas of the mountains.

The plan was to ride up a trail about 6 or 7 miles on horses, set up camp, and then hunt the first day and a half of the season. Then ride out with two nice bucks. "Piece of cake," he told me. It didn't quite work out like that. I should have known.

I had never ridden a horse before this trip. I should have been smart enough to not have done my first one with Ted.

He borrowed a horse for me from a friend of his. He loaded both horses and our gear into his horse hauling truck and away we went early one morning heading for the east side of the Cascade Mountains. We arrived at the trailhead and unloaded the horses and gear. I loaded my rifle and gear into a backpack and put it on. I don't remember what he carried his meager stuff in, but it didn't amount to much.

He told me to saddle my horse while he saddled his. I told him that I knew less than zero about how that was done, so he put my saddle on also. I tried to mount the horse and then realized that my hiking boots would not fit into the foot things, which I believe are called stirrups. He thought that was pretty funny that I had to ride the whole way with my feet just hanging down without using the stirrups. I didn't think it was funny at all.

Anyway, we headed up the mountain and eventually came to a large meadow, where we made camp, such as it was. Camp was mostly a small somewhat flat area with a slight incline on top of a small hill. We laid our sleeping bags on the bare ground, no tent, no sleeping pads, just the bare ground. I had thought ahead enough to bring a small 6'x6' piece of plastic to lay my bag on with a small overlap to cover it with. Ted had no protective covering.

When we had first ridden into camp, we had spotted a couple of deer across the meadow which gave us high hopes for the next day. We ate our peanut butter and jam sandwiches for dinner and went to bed soon after dusk with nothing but wonderful thoughts of what tomorrow would bring.

Sometime during the night, I awoke with rain hitting me in the face. I just pulled the plastic a little higher so it covered my head and went blissfully back to sleep. Sometime later, I awoke again, to the sound of a fire and Ted rustling around above me. Since he had no cover for his sleeping bag, he had gotten quite wet and cold. So, he had gotten up and built this dandy little fire, just slightly above me and was trying to get warm.

I again drifted off in slumberland only to be abruptly woken up when a small burning log rolled away from the fire and jammed against my sleeping bag. It immediately burned most of the plastic off me before I could get the log off. Hence, I was soon sitting beside the fire with my buddy, and soon became just as wet as him.

We stuck it out by that fire until dawn and decided that hunting deer wasn't quite as important as survival. We were at an elevation of about 7 thousand feet in the middle of September and it was darn cold, especially being as wet as we were.

We saddled up the horses, put what little we had in our wet backpacks, and got ready to head back down the mountain to the truck and home without doing a lick of hunting.

Ted had made me saddle my own horse and cinch it up myself against my better judgment. I knew better, but did as I was told. He mounted his horse and I mounted mine.

As soon as I swung up onto the saddle with my pack on, the saddle and I and all my gear, including my rifle, immediately ended up underneath the horse. Apparently, I had not tightened the cinch enough, which I found out later. The saddle and I had slid off his back, around his side and under his belly. The saddle was facing the ground and me laying there in the mud.

Ted again, thought this was one of the funniest things he had ever seen and almost fell off his horse because of laughing so hard. I thought I might have seen a snicker on the horse's face also. I never could find any humor in any of this. I again swore for about the 100th time that if I survived this trip, I would never, ever have anything to do with my "friend" Ted again, ever.

He finally recovered enough to dismount and properly reinstall my saddle, or so I thought. We eventually remounted and headed down the trail, and everything seemed to be going quite well for the first mile or two. For whatever reason, my horse would stop at every trickle of water that crossed the trail and take a drink. He would bend over with his head and neck bending forward and down while doing this. With the heavy rain, there were a lot of trickles. I was somewhat nervous about it at first, but all seemed well.

After about two miles and a dozen or so drinks later, we came to a bit larger trickle, actually a small stream. Mr. Horse bent over for another drink and I felt the saddle slip forward a little bit. The horse shuddered a little bit with his head still down, and away I went again. This time, the saddle slid forward onto his neck, and the pack and I went right over his neck and head into the stream.

This time I thought for sure my "old friend Ted", was going to die, either from a heart attack from laughing so hard, he could barely breath, or else when I could get my hands on him. He is a very sick man to find so much humor in such a thing as this.

That ended it. I had had enough. Never, ever, ever, ever, again, would I ride or attempt to ride a horse again. It's been over 50 years since that episode and I am still holding to my oath. I am not real smart, but even I figured out horses were not meant to ride if Ted had anything at all to do with the trip.

I walked the last 4 miles off that mountain, and again vowed I would never have anything at all to do with anything involving horses again. There can be no reasonable reason at all on God's green earth, to ever break that vow.

I should have included Ted in that vow, also.

CHAPTER 17

LESSONS LEARNED and to be LEARNED

If a person has hunted as many years as I have, and hasn't gained experience and skills, about both hunting and life, there must be something wrong with them. Some hunters think that the whole hunting experience is about driving to the woods somewhere, walk a little bit, (if they have to), shoot a record book animal, clean it, stuff it in your vehicle, bring it to a butcher, pick it up a week or so later, eat it if your mate will cook it, and then brag about it for years to come. There is much more to hunting than that.

I have had many wonderful experiences on most of my hunting trips. It seems as though I am always learning new skills about hunting, and about life in general, and about this wonderful planet we live on.

Five stories come to mind. The first three are about learning new hunting skills. The fourth one is about how stupid I am about paying attention to facts already learned. The fifth story is about how essential it is to plan ahead.

One of the first lessons I learned was taught to me by my then, five- year old son, Marc. During my first years of hunting with my father at his Oak Creek camp, we would leave home very early on the Friday morning before opening day of deer season, which was always on a Saturday. We would drive about 3 ½ hours from home (Port Orchard), to the camp site and then set up the whole camp by afternoon. We would then locate one or more dead tamarack trees, cut them down and into the proper lengths for firewood. We would then bring them back to camp, have dinner and go to bed early so we would be ready for the next day's hunt. This was always a fun and satisfying experience for all of us. When my wife, Elaine, and both the children, Marc and Nicki, were along it was even better. It was truly a real- life adventure for them. Both children started coming along on the opening weekend trips when they were about 3 to 5 years old and did so for many years afterward. In fact, even now that they are both in their forties, they still come along when they can, even though neither of them hunt.

Right from the get go, I always took Marc with me on opening morning, and eventually Nicki started traipsing along also. I never ever shot anything while they were along, but it was worth every unproductive moment. We had such a great time and memorable experiences while learning more about outdoor life and about each other. We made a lot of noise, which probably contributed to our lack of game, but that was absolutely OK.

One humorous thing about Marc, was that he was so concerned about getting lost in the woods, that he always stayed about one step behind me. When sneaking along through the woods, I learned to not stop too suddenly or he would step on my heels. When I say he was only one step behind, that is exactly what I mean. It took a couple of years before he gained enough courage to follow at a reasonable distance.

Well, on one of those hunts, we were following an animal trail through some thick reprod, when he suddenly whispered to me, "Daddy, there's a deer." I quickly looked around and saw nothing but trees. I then looked down at him and said "Where is it?" He pointed in the direction of the deer, and so I looked very carefully in the direction he was pointing, and still saw nothing but trees.

I again looked down at him and said, "Are you sure it's a deer?" I also noticed that his eyes were huge and very excited looking. He said, "Yes, right over there.", pointing again to the same spot.

I looked again and still saw nothing but trees. I thought about it for a couple more seconds and then it dawned on me that Marc, being only about 5 or6 years old was about 2 ½ feet shorter than me. I then kneeled down to his eye level and so was able to look under the branches of the nearby trees, and sure enough, there was a deer feeding along only about 50 or 60 feet away. I was only able to spot it by kneeling down so as to be able to see under the branches of the trees.

I just wonder how much game has been passed by, by not taking the time and being in too much of a hurry, to look everywhere possible before proceeding on ones' way. What a great lesson taught to me by my young son.

Incidentally, that deer was a doe, and so was illegal to shoot, but it could have just as well been a buck.

The next lesson is again about observation. When sitting or standing in a blind, make sure you look all around you, not just in the obvious direction you would most likely expect to see game. Don't just look straight ahead, but also to both sides and even in back of you, even though the chance of seeing game might be somewhat slim.

It was the opening morning of deer season, maybe 25 years ago. I was hunting out of our Oak Creek camp and had left camp well before light so I could drop down onto what we call Joe's Canyon Ridge to a large rock about ¾ mile from camp. I was planning on establishing myself on the rock that overlooked both a large part of Joe's Canyon and a large area below the rock. I figured that would be an excellent spot for opening morning, because of hunters coming up the hill from the Tieton Pond area and from also the White Pass Hwy.

Great plan, but you know how that often goes!

I was just getting to within about 100 yards of that rock and just above it as it got light enough to see clearly. Lo and behold, someone had beat me to that rock. He must have come up from below, and had left mighty early to have gotten there before me. I was quite shocked and also very disappointed to see him there. I had never before seen another hunter at that spot before that time. Now I would have to plan a completely different hunt and it was already getting light. Darn! I stood above him for a couple of minutes trying to figure out what to do next. He never looked my way and so had no idea I was even in the area.

Then something very interesting and kind of exciting happened.

A coyote came running from my right side about half way between that other hunter and myself. He took a sharp right turn and ran directly towards that other hunter, who was just standing looking over and down off the rock. The coyote came to within about 20 feet of him before either smelling or spotting him. The coyote, being suddenly surprised at being so close to that other gent, leaped in the air and changed direction in one motion and headed directly up the hill towards me. He ran right by my right side and passed within about 10 feet of me. I had remained absolutely motionless. I thought, "How neat was that."

Then all of a sudden, another coyote came running from the same area the first one had come from, and also headed down towards that other guy, saw him, changed directions and ran up towards me, passing within about 10 feet of me on my left side.

Instantly after that, a 3rd coyote came from the same area as the other two and did the same thing as both of them did. He also ran up and past me.

I stood there awhile longer, looking down towards that other hunter and you know what? He never ever looked behind him while I was there. He never saw me or any of those three critters that had come so close to him.

I thought to myself, "Shame on him for missing the circus that had just happened so close to him."

The lesson being, observe all around you, not just in front. It doesn't take a great deal of effort to swivel your neck once in a while. It might make the difference between eating venison or just your tag. You can figure out which one tastes better.

The next lesson learned is one that many new hunters are guilty of. Anyone that has talked to an experienced hunter, or read any hunting magazine should know about this rule. The rule is; sight your rifle in BEFORE hunting, EVERY year.

Many years ago, about the time I started getting serious about big game hunting, I bought a used 30-06 rifle, and also a new Leopold scope to mount on it.

I didn't get the rifle and scope to the gunsmith, and I say gunsmith with a question mark, until less than a week before season. My brother, Jerry and I were planning on hunting the Jumpoff Joe area above Rimrock Lake, which is just to the south of Hwy. 12 on the White Pass Hwy. The gunsmith was supposed to mount and boresight the new scope, which shouldn't have been too great of a task for a professional.

I picked the rifle up late in the afternoon on the evening we were to leave on our trip. I have to say that all this was partially my fault for procrastinating so long to get the scope mounted. Anyway, I figured that I had time to do the final sighting in before dark. Wrong!

I quickly drove out to the local gravel pit, set up a target at 100 yards and proceeded to send a couple of shots towards it. Since it was bore sighted, my first 2 shots were fairly close to the center, but not close enough to my satisfaction. I adjusted the crosshairs a couple of clicks and sent off two more rounds. The second two shots were a little further away from the bull than the first two. "What the heck is going on", I say to myself. I again adjusted the scope another couple of clicks and pounded off a couple more shots, and guess what, they were even further from the bull. By then it was too dark to shoot anymore, and I was thoroughly confused. I then met Jerry, and we headed over to the other side of the Cascade Mtns., set up camp and went to bed. We got up early and were out of camp before light.

I had planned on hunting until about noon and then setting up a target and try to figure out what the problem was. I also figured that the gun was sighted in enough for a fairly close shot.

About 10 AM that morning, I was pussyfooting along a side hill looking down into and across a small wooded canyon. I spotted a nice two-point buck directly across the canyon about 150 yards away as the crow flies. He was just walking along, giving me plenty of time to lay down and take a careful aim. I aimed just slightly behind the right front shoulder and squeezed the trigger. He dropped immediately, and I thought "all right". But then I saw him trying to stand up. I absolutely hate to see an animal in agony. It's against everything I hold dear. So, I started shooting at his head to finish him off. I shot the other 5 shots but could not hit him again, even though he was barely moving. I quickly reloaded and ran down the canyon and up the other side to where he was. I quickly shot him in the head to finish him. I was appalled to see that my first shot from across the canyon had broken both front legs just below the body.

I have to say that, especially in my younger years, I was an excellent shot when I had a rest, which I did at that first shot, and then to have missed all those head shots, I knew that my scope was dreadfully out of adjustment.

I was very, very upset about the whole episode. I almost cried thinking about how that poor deer must have suffered. It upset me so much that I quit hunting for two years. Secondly, I was very upset with that gunsmith for mounting that scope in some sort of goofy way to make it shoot so haywire. Thirdly, I was very upset with myself for procrastinating so long to buy the gun and scope and not having the time to get it sighted in properly.

As it turned out, the next day after packing the deer out and back to camp, we set up a target to get it sighted in properly. We found out that the gunsmith had the scope ¼ turn off from what it was supposed to be. So, when you adjusted the scope right or left, it would move the bullet up or down. If you adjusted the scope up or down, it would move the bullet left or right.

The lesson being: do not go hunting until you are SURE your rifle is sighted in correctly.

I have heard many other similar and sad stories from other hunters. Don't be one of them.

The fourth story is to confirm the fact of how stupid I am. I have never been accused of being too bright, and this story shows why. Maybe twenty or so years ago, I shot a nice grouse with my pistol while bear hunting. I gutted, defeathered, and dismembered the feet and what was left of the head and placed it in my cooler, so Elaine could cook it up for us upon my return home.

A couple days later I got home, and Elaine applied her magic to that bird, and we had it for supper. It was perfectly cooked and tasted as good as any grouse can be. I believe I ate the wings first and then cut open the breast about where the neck connects to it and took a big bite. To my horror, my mouth filled up with something even I knew wasn't meat. I immediately spit it out onto my plate. I took a close look at what had come out of my mouth and discovered a pile of mostly pine needles. It didn't take a rocket scientist to realize that I had forgotten to remove the craw when butchering that grouse. I have butchered my share of birds and so have no excuse for leaving that craw in that bird.

Lesson number four--- do not leave the craw in a bird or you will not appreciate the consequences.

The fifth lesson is about planning ahead and knowing the geography and topography of the area you plan on hunting.

In 1961, my friend, Paul Schlenker and I had been working a summer job in the hop fields near the town of Moxee City, Wash. We had worked the whole month of September and the first part of October until the beginning of deer season. We had both heard that it was excellent mule deer hunting in the mountains near the town of Entiat, Wash. Neither of us had been in that area before this trip, but we decided to give it a try on opening weekend.

We drove there the day before opening, and came to the Entiat River. We drove along it until we came to a spot we could wade across. We both had our backpacks, sleeping bags and a limited amount of gear. We had brought some canned food and little else.

No water at all. We were used to hunting and hiking in Western Washington, where there is rarely any shortage of water.

It was a hot afternoon when we waded that river and climbed to the top of that mountain, where we expected to find either a pond or small stream. Our plan was to be on top of that mountain on opening morning, and all the hunters coming up from the bottom would drive a couple of nice bucks right to us. Piece of cake we thought.

Well, so much for our wonderful planning. There was not a drop of water on that hill or anywhere close by, except back down the way we had come. By the time we had reached the top, it was dusk and we would have sold our mothers for one cold cup of water. We decided to forego our dinner, because of having no moisture to get it down our gullets. We threw our bags on the ground and tried to get a night's sleep. Have you ever tried to sleep when your throat was so dry it hurt? Not very fun or successful. We were absolutely miserable.

As soon as it was light enough for us to travel, we threw our bags in the packs and beat feet off that miserable dry mountain as fast as we could. That river, a couple of miles below us, was the only thing on our tiny little minds. We had seen a couple of deer the day before on our way up, but as fast and as noisy as we were descending, we saw nary one deer or any other living thing.

We cared less! The only thing on our puny minds was that cold running water in that wonderful life- giving river just below us.

When we finally hit the bottom of that hill and came to the river, all I remember doing was dropping my pack and rifle and diving in, clothes, boots and all. Now I know what heaven on earth feels like. It was just about the most wonderful thing that ever was, when we hit that cold, wet, beautiful water.

We hung out in that river for quite a while until we were pretty sure we were going to survive, before we walked out, grabbed our packs and rifles, waded across to the car and headed for home.

Lesson learned: don't take things for granted.

Don't just concentrate on a few exciting details, plan for any unforeseen circumstances. A good topo map with all the necessary details such as water availability or lack of, would have made all the difference between a successful hunt or the disastrous one we experienced.

CHAPTER 18

THE PAST SIX or EIGHT YEARS to PRESENT

I started writing this book about eight or ten years ago, probably about the year 2010 or so, and hope to finish it this year, 2019. Since I began writing all those years ago, several things have changed.

The most significant changes are that I have lost both my dear brother, Jerry, and friend, Jim Eagleton, both to cancer, and longtime friend, Bob Wilson retired and moved to Montana, which I have mentioned in a previous chapter.

Jerry passed in 2014, Jim in 2015, and Bob moved in 2010. It is amazing how much these two deaths and Bobs' moving have changed my life.

Brother Jerry had such a stabilizing effect on my whole life. Being two years older, he was my protector, mentor, instructor, best friend, and most of all, he was an example on how to live my life. He was my "go to guy" throughout my whole life.

Jim was an especially great friend. We met many years ago when our wives, Elaine and Peggy, became best of friends. Our children were all about the same ages, and also became good friends. We all shared many fun times and adventures together. When he passed, that left only Bill and I together at elk camp with occasional visits from Wesley, (Bobs' son and Bills' nephew).

Life is still good, but not like it used to be.

For the past eight years or so, I hunt deer almost exclusively near the town of St. John, Wash. I hunt with my wife's cousin, Bill Wright and his son Greg, and son-in-law, Cory Crews. Several other of Bills' friends and family have joined us occasionally. We stay on a farm owned by dear friends, Joe and Sara Delong. The farm borders the

Palouse River and has been in Joes' family for many, many years. We stay in the bunkhouse, which has a full bathroom, including a shower, a complete kitchen, and can sleep up to about six or seven.

On Sunday mornings or afternoons, we try to be back to the bunkhouse to watch the Seahawks play, depending at what time the game is.

We hunt mostly on Joe and Sara's farm and the neighboring farm owned by a man named Carlos. Occasionally we drive to another farm owned by a man named Dennis. Both Carlos and Dennis have been very accommodating to us and are much appreciated. Nice guys. Bill and his crew have been doing this hunt for over 20 years. I was invited to join them about 8 years ago and have not missed getting my deer yet. The first year I hunted with them, it took me about one minute to bag a nice 4- point muley. It's too late to get rid of me now.

We always gut our deer immediately after being shot, but usually don't skin them until we are back on the farm. We then use Joes' tractor to lift them up and do the skinning and wash the body cavity out. We then wrap them in either old bed sheets or game bags, and then hang them in the barn for cooling until we head for home. For a couple of years, there were about seven or eight of us hunting on the farm and it took us only about three or four days to limit out. It was pretty impressive to see that many deer hanging at the same location, especially since most of them were three point or better bucks. In this hunt area, if the hunter is 65 or older, he has the option of shooting a whitetail doe instead of a three point or better buck. There are both muley and whitetail deer in the area, but the whitetails outnumber the muleys about five to one.

To earn our keep on the farm, we try to help Joe and Sara with some of the farm chores. We have dug both potatoes and postholes, stacked hay bales, castrated both pigs and cattle, cut, split, and stacked several log truck loads of firewood, and other misc. tasks. Sara is a great cook and feeds us dinner most nights, but we pretty much fend for ourselves at breakfast and lunch. The refrigerator is very well stocked with both beverages and snacks.

I would probably still be hunting deer at our Oak Creek camp except it is such poor deer hunting now, compared with what it used to be, since our beloved game department shortened and changed the season. It is so early now that we miss out on all the migratory deer that used to flood the area when the snow moved them out of the high country. It is amazing what a week or two makes at that time of year. Without the migratory deer, there are only a few local deer around that have been hunted very hard. Not many left. There are way fewer hunting camps now than there used to be. Others such as myself have relocated to more productive areas.

We used to get our bucks almost every year, but not anymore. I believe that my partner Bill, who still hunts there with his friend Brian Dahl, has not connected in five or six years. Even the Whitehouse camp that ticketed out for 30 or more years has gotten blanked a couple of years since the season change. I feel quite lucky to have found an area to fill my tag every year.

I still hunt elk at Oak Creek every year with Bill, and enjoy that very much.

I haven't hunted bear for several years, but did pass up a shot at a young bear while elk hunting a few years ago. It was about a three-year- old, pure black and as rolly polly as they get. It looked like it didn't miss many dinners. It was just meandering back and forth below the Flattop until it waddled under a tree and took a siesta. It was just too darned cute to shoot.

I am finishing the writing of this book in June of 2019 and have just found out that I drew a cow tag in the lottery and my partner Bill, drew an any bull tag, and his daughter Taylor, drew a cow tag also. Also, Don Whitehouse from the camp below us drew a cow tag. If we don't fill our freezers this year, we had better retire to a nursing home. Stay tuned.

Results of the season - I got my cow on the first day of cow season. I took Taylor, Bill's daughter, to the same clearing the next morning. She shot her first elk"a cow" within about 100 feet of where I got mine, about 20 minutes after watching a large couger walking through. Not enough time to get a shot at it though.

Several days later, Craig from the Vashon Camp saw a bear visiting out gut piles, but he didn't have a bear tag. Bill and Don ate thier tags.

Typical hunting success on the Delong Ranch.
(left to right) Myself, Greg, Cory and Bill.

CHAPTER 19

FUN and INTERESTING THINGS

If a person spends much time hunting, fishing, hiking, or really anything, he will eventually experience a multitude of things that are out of the ordinary. Here are a few of mine that don't quite fit into any of the other chapters.

Many years ago, I was deer hunting at Oak Creek, and had dropped down from camp to a relatively flat area below what we call "the Flattop". I was moving slowly along, about to leave a shale slide to a wooded area. I glanced to my left and saw a movement about 100 feet away. I stood and watched it for a few seconds and soon realized that what I was seeing, was a porcupine. He was scurrying along about a quarter mile an hour. I walked over to it and got to within about 10 feet of it, before he saw me. He immediately stuck his head under a nearby log and had his tail pointed towards me. I was sharp enough to know to not get too close to his missile system. I actually have a sometimes- workable brain, although there are those that might argue with me about that.

I stood real still for a while until he lifted his head and glanced to both sides until he saw me again, at which time he immediately stuck his head under the log again. The stories of how ostriches stick their heads in the sand, came to mind. He did this another time or two, until I finally decided to leave him to his own agenda and I to mine.

The second story is about ticks.

Maybe about 2008 or so, I was on my first whitetail hunt near the town of Deer Park, Wash. I had failed to get my buck during the regular season at Oak Creek, and so was hunting a late hunt near Deer Park. I had never hunted that area before, so had to search around a bit to find a legal area to hunt, since most of the area was private farm lands with "No Hunting" signs posted.

I finally found a wooded area with no signs posted, parked my truck and quickly headed up into the woods, since it was already late afternoon. I hadn't been in the woods long, before I was flagged by a couple of whitetails. I had heard about how they will raise their tails and wave them goodbye to you, but had not experienced this before. It was somewhat of an exciting experience for me.

Eventually, I spotted a nice 3-point whitetail and put the kibosh on him. It was only about half an hour before dark. I quickly gutted him and started dragging him downhill towards my truck. It was well after dark before I reached the truck. I threw him on a tarp in the bed, and headed for home (Port Orchard).

I arrived home the next morning and immediately hung and skinned him in my garage. When I cut the tail off, I realized how pretty and fluffy it was. I stuffed it in a plastic bag to show Elaine, later.

The next day, I went out to the garage with Elaine to show her how pretty a whitetails tail is. I opened the bag and pulled the tail out and was shocked to see it covered with ticks. I think I counted about 14 or so before putting it back in the bag. I immediately carried it down to the bay and cast it into the sea. The bag was burned as soon as I could do it. I've seen ticks on other game before, but never so many.

My third story is about my friend Ted Schmitz, and his calamity. He was also the star of chapter 16. He is the guy with the weird sense of humor, who tricked me into that horrendous horse ride written about in that same chapter. He has a way of being in the middle of trouble. This story is a sort of payback he got for abusing me so much in chap. 16. In 1999, Ted, his son, Gary and four other friends were on the early high deer hunt in the Wash. Cascade Mountains.

They always ride their horses in about 26 miles and set up camp about 5 to 7 days before opening day of the season, which is always Sept. 15. This gives them time to get some high-lake fishing and scout the area for deer. They camp on Border Ridge which is less than a mile from the Canadian border.

After a day or so in camp, they rode their horses, with a mule in tow, to Tungsten Lake, which is about 12 miles from their base camp. They stayed there a day or two, to indulge in some excellent trout fishing. Two days before deer opening, they packed up and headed back towards base camp.

After travelling only about a mile or so, they came upon a large flat rock that dropped off a couple of feet on the downhill side. Ted was leading the group with his mule in tow. When he came to the rock, his horse was reluctant to step off of it. After hesitating a bit, it sort of jumped off the rock. When the rope, between Ted and the mule became taut, (the mule had also stopped on the rock as the horse had), it jerked Ted up and out of his saddle a couple of feet. With Ted in the air, the mule then decided to also jump off the rock as the horse had done. The pressure now off of the lead rope, resulted in Ted dropping back into the saddle.

Gary, his son, who was riding directly behind him heard a loud "pop", when Teds' crotch hit the saddle. This was not a good thing. Ted, who was the first one to the scene of the accident, knew it was not a good thing before anybody else. He was in instant pain.

Still in the saddle, he continued down the trail for a short distance. The pain didn't subside, so he figured that if he got off the horse, there might be less pain. He somehow got down off the horse and realized that he could not take even one step. He could stand up but not move his feet at all.

He then somehow got back on the horse and rode all the way to base camp, which was about 10 miles. This was not a pleasant or easy task. Along the way three events happened that made it even more painful. The first was encountering a sow and cub bear, which caused the horse to jerk and jump around which was much worse than the usual bump and grind of a back-country ride. The second event was flushing a grouse which caused the same results as the bears had. The third was the horse stepping in a gopher hole, which in turn caused the same horrid jumping around. It's a good thing Ted is a very tough guy, even though not too smart.

They finally made it to base camp, where Ted had to get off his trusty steed. He still could not walk, so had to crawl everywhere he went. He first crawled over to the side a bit to eliminate bodily liquids, while lying on his side. He then crawled into the tent.

Someone with a low I.Q. rating, such as myself, might have found it a bit funny watching him lying on his side while peeing. I believe that he did not find it funny at all.

He took notice of what he was doing and determined that he was not passing blood and figured that as a good sign. He was extremely swollen in the groin area, but found that once he was in the tent laying down there was little or no pain.

They all went to bed, laying on the ground, but during the night an odd thing kept happening. Every so often his right leg would just kind of drift over and into Garys' side. This kept happening until they put a piece of firewood against the meandering leg. Weird!

By morning, it was unanimous that Ted was less than useless and needed to be helicoptered out. One of the guys rode about 3 miles or so to a sheepherder's cabin where a forest ranger was staying. He radioed down to the main ranger station and requested a helicopter evacuation. The chopper arrived and transported him to the hospital in Omak, Wash. Ted asked them to take him straight to Harborview Hospital in Seattle, but for whatever reason they declined to do it.

In the Omak hospital, they did their diagnosis and determined that he had split his pelvis in half. OUCH! There was some talk of waiting a day or two before operating on him, but Ted told them if they did not do the operation that day, he would check out and have his wife, Sandy, drive him across the mountains to Seattle for the procedure.

The doctor was not very pleased with Teds' decision, and against his own judgment, he did the operation that very day. They joined his pelvis back together with a plate and four screws.

He and Sandy left the very next day, driving over the mountains and back home. Like I've said before, Ted is no sissy. He was lucky that his insurance paid all but $500 of his medical expenses.

My fourth story is about our dear friend Nancy Mc Abee, and the drastic steps she took to get her name in my book. Nancy and I went thru high school together, graduating from South Kitsap High School in the class of 1960. She was smart, gorgeous, very nice, and in the popular group of our class. I was in the other group of kids that you might call the low lifes. I hung out with Ted and others just like him, but Nancy and I were friends anyway.

Well, over the years, Nancy became very good friends with Elaine. They are in the local chapter of a guild that supports the Children's Orthopedic Hospital in Seattle. They also spend a lot of time yakking and doing other important womens' things.

One day, they were rummaging around in our den, doing what, I don't know, but Nancy was bending over and when she raised up, she impaled the top of her head on a brow tine of a set of moose antlers that were hanging on the wall. We have normal 8- foot ceilings, but when you have a set of horns that are 57 inches across and about 3 ½ feet high, that only leaves about 4 ½ feet from the floor to the lower brow tines. I don't know Nancys' exact height, but I do know it is more than 4 ½ feet. That fact wasn't a good thing!

As Elaine and I were trying to stem the flow of blood, she looked up at me with very sad eyes and said, "Will this get me in your hunting book".

The answer is yes, and believe it or not we are still friends.

Myself on stand in camp. A bonfire, my rifle, binoculars, bag of peanuts, cold beverage, and a good book. It doesn't get much better than this.

www.ingramcontent.com/pod-product-compliance
Lightning Source LLC
Chambersburg PA
CBHW052146110526
44591CB00012B/1875